FLIP THE SCRIPT

FLIP THE SCRIPT

Getting People to Think
Your Idea Is Their Idea

—

OREN KLAFF

with Andy Earle

PORTFOLIO / PENGUIN

Portfolio/Penguin
An imprint of Penguin Random House LLC
penguinrandomhouse.com

Most Portfolio books are available at a discount when purchased in quantity
for sales promotions or corporate use. Special editions, which include personalized
covers, excerpts, and corporate imprints, can be created when purchased in
large quantities. For more information, please call (212) 572-2232 or email
specialmarkets@penguinrandomhouse.com. Your local bookstore can also assist
with discounted bulk purchases using the Penguin Random House corporate
Business-to-Business program. For assistance in locating a participating
retailer, email B2B@penguinrandomhouse.com.

ISBN 9780525533948 (hardcover)
ISBN 9780525533955 (ebook)

Printed in Canada
1   3   5   7   9   10   8   6   4   2

Book design by Cassandra Garruzzo

Some names and identifying characteristics have been changed to protect
the privacy of the individuals involved.

While the author has made every effort to provide accurate telephone numbers, internet
addresses, and other contact information at the time of publication, neither the publisher
nor the author assumes any responsibility for errors, or for changes that occur after
publication. Further, the publisher does not have any control over and does not assume
any responsibility for author or third-party websites or their content.

*For Mom. Your spirited writing style and irreverent
storytelling are the DNA of this book.*

CONTENTS

Here's the big idea in 81 words:

I don't like being pressured into making a purchase. And I'm not alone. Over decades of being marketed, pitched, sold, and lied to, we've all grown resistant to sales persuasion. The moment we feel pressured to buy, we pull away. And if we're told what to do or what to think, our defenses go up. In other words, buyers don't put much trust in you and your ideas. However, everyone trusts their own ideas.

Accordingly, today, products are bought, not sold.

If you're trying to make a deal in this environment, it's never been harder. Buyers in your industry are skeptical of new products and services, and if you're the person who has to sell to them, they'll be skeptical of you as well. They fact-check everything you say, sometimes while you're saying it. And buyers are always looking for a better deal, thinking they can somehow improve on your offer, no matter how good it is.

Instead of pushing your idea on the buyer, it's a better move to guide them to discover it on their own, so they believe it, trust it, and get excited about it. Then they'll *want* to buy it and will feel good about the chance to work with you.

This book is dedicated to showing you how to plant your idea in the mind of another so they will discover it, appreciate it, and fall in love with it on their own. But you cannot accomplish this with standard sales methods. Instead, you need to flip the script.

I'M OREN KLAFF. Several years ago, I wrote a book called *Pitch Anything*, in which I taught readers a unique method to prepare and deliver a pitch that would wow buyers and investors every time. It was a method I'd developed for myself in the world of tech, but it proved to be incredibly useful for others as well. As word spread about the effectiveness of *Pitch Anything*, soon over a million people were using it in their everyday business, and before I knew it, I was getting calls from people at companies like Google, Amazon, and Bank of America telling me how useful they'd found my method.

Next, companies from Germany, Italy, and Russia were calling. The result: I was being invited to help pitch large deals in far-flung parts of the world. I'd never imagined my ideas would travel so far from Silicon Valley.

In the years since I wrote *Pitch Anything*, the marketplace has changed. **Buyers have become more cold and digital, and so I**

have changed with them, creating new methods for closing deals. These new methods are what I've put in this book.

Bluntly, here's the problem: Enthusiastic sellers make an impressive pitch but then quickly switch over to "closing mode," applying just the kind of unwanted pressure that blows up deals these days faster than you can say "Sign here." Or aspiring sellers will make the world's greatest pitch and then stop, unsure of what to do next, hoping the deal will come through all on its own.

Both these approaches are the norm, and painful to watch. For that reason, I developed a revolutionary approach, a way to win every deal without spending a single moment selling or trying to close—a way to sell without selling at all. In other words, the buyer feels it's his or her idea to work with you and makes the deal happen. You don't apply pressure, try to overcome objections, or give chase.

So here's what I want you to understand right from the beginning of this book. Closing a deal without sales pressure is not a mystery. It's not some superpower that certain people have and others don't. Getting a deal done is a step-by-step process and it's available to anybody who knows how to follow a few basic rules. Because once you know the rules, you never have to push someone to close; instead, you can make them feel like they came up with your idea themselves, which leads a deal to close naturally, as if it were always meant to happen. This ability to *flip the script* will help you in any situation and close any deal.

In this book, I'm going to teach you those rules and show you the steps to persuade your prospects without pressuring them.

First, I'll introduce the idea of Inception—planting an idea in someone else's brain. From there, I'll show you how to use the Dominance Hierarchy and the rules of Certainty to turn the tables and put yourself in a position of strength, instead of the buyer holding all the cards. Next, I'll demonstrate the power of a Pre-Wired Idea and how to make your deal feel Plain Vanilla, like it's the most normal and obvious thing in the world—in other words, something your prospect's mind can easily grasp. Then you'll discover how to use the buyer's natural Pessimism as a force in your favor, and how to be Compelling when it matters most. Finally, you'll get to see how all these ideas work together as I describe in detail what can only be called "the deal of a lifetime."

To protect the confidentiality of my clients and more effectively illustrate how you can apply these ideas, I've changed many identifying details of people and companies involved and fictionalized some aspects of the stories. Nonetheless, every one of these examples is based on a real-life business deal in which I used these techniques effectively.

For example, let me tell you about the time I tried to sell a $10 million software deal to one of the most powerful men in Russia.

FLIP THE SCRIPT

CHAPTER 1

Why You Need Inception

he truly rich in Russia are called oligarchs, a term that has come to mean control, power, and ruthlessness. And Viktor [last name redacted] definitely deserves the title. His luxurious office sits atop a high rise overlooking the Moscow River. Viktor sits behind a presidential desk, wearing a tourbillion watch that I recognize from a popular gear and gadgets website, list price $1 million. Every wall in this office is decorated with photos of oil rigs, factories, container ships, and cargo planes he presumably owns; over his desk is a massive and oddly beautiful painting of an oil refinery with a caption engraved in brass, NOVOGROD #12. Viktor is heavyset, tall, and burly—in another life he might have been a rugby player. His smile isn't a smile at all. The executives of all his companies fear him, and I fear him too.

There are three things you need to know about doing deals

with Russian oligarchs. Number one, they aren't interested in losing money—ever, under any circumstances. Second, they don't make emotional decisions; Russians are raised on a steady diet of math, physics, engineering, and electronics, and they analyze every decision ten different ways, then have a shot of vodka and analyze it one more time. Third, you simply cannot lose an oligarch's money and say, "Yikes, sorry it didn't work, but I tried really hard," like you can in Silicon Valley. Instead, you need to do whatever it takes to get their money back.

So, if there's a World Championship of Dealmaking, this is it.

Why would I ever leave my comfortable Los Angeles office to travel across the world to participate in this kind of stress-inducing meeting?

MicroGenetics, the company I represented, needed to hire a dozen or more PhD mathematicians, but in the United States, these are a very rare and expensive commodity. Competent mathematicians easily command a million dollars per contract on the global exchange, and that was way over the company's budget. In Russia, however, you can still find skilled but affordable mathematicians, but not without a powerful local sponsor. Viktor was a man who could wave his finger and get us whatever we wanted. Bottom line, my client needed both his money and his approval in order to navigate the layers of bureaucracy that come with any deal in Russia.

This is how I found myself standing on the fifty-ninth floor of a tower in downtown Moscow, in an office that felt more like an exhibit at the Getty museum than a place of business. I was flanked on each side by translators and analysts, eager to get rid of me and keep Viktor on his precise daily schedule.

My presentation was just getting underway, but I was already in serious trouble. At first, Viktor was listening to me with great interest, nodding his head in comprehension as I explained our genetic sequencing technology that we believed would save millions of lives and revolutionize health care. When I paused to take a quick breath, he jumped in to criticize my deal in perfect English: "Your software code has many syntax and computational errors." But when I countered that point, describing a rock-solid contract we had with a major US tech firm, proving the technology worked, Viktor stared at me blankly, needing his translator to explain each word, even then looking distant and lost.

Back and forth we went like this. Every question he shot at me was forceful and articulate and from the mind of a brilliant investor. Every answer I gave was met with a blank stare. Then Viktor would say, "Please you explain this more better," and translators would step in for a long, drawn-out exchange that went nowhere.

I had to explain our technology to him in the same way I might show my elderly neighbor how to send a text message. "Human genetic data is like millions of grains of sand," I said, using a weird analogy I had just made up. Next I was using gestures that looked like hand puppets to help make this point.

Viktor cut me off: "That makes no sense."

Oh god. He was right. It didn't. Now my mouth was saying things my brain hadn't approved of yet.

I was losing control of this deal. But I had to keep moving

forward. So I launched into the most exciting part of my pitch, explaining the revolutionary new features that set us apart in the world of genetic data.

Just before I finished, Viktor turned away from me, ignoring what I was saying. With his back to me, he spoke in Russian to his team of advisers for a few minutes. I didn't know if I was supposed to leave, wait quietly, or perform a magic trick.

Finally, he turned back to me, a little surprised I was still there. His eyes narrowed in an unfriendly way; then, when I opened my mouth to say something, he smiled broadly, waving his hand to cut me off. "Yes, yes, we know all this," he said, and looked at me as if I were a boring commercial you have to watch before the real show begins.

Viktor had taken away all my usual control points. He was using his power and a supposed language barrier to put me into a low-status position. I was acting needy and anxious, and negotiating against myself. This was a dealmaker's nightmare. I knew he was going to make an offer, because I was still in the room, but I also knew the terms of the deal would be horrendous.

As this unfolded, I was watching myself fall back onto the classic sales approach, with its tired old script: First become likable and build rapport, then explain "features and benefits," next do a trial close, and then fight like an alley cat to overcome all the objections the buyer has come up with.

Russian oligarchs do *not* like being sold this way or argued with, especially by Americans. And Viktor is definitely no exception to this rule. He has a big mustache, which the President of

Russia once suggested he shave off because it looked too "Soviet." He said *nyet* to that request, and *nyet* to virtually every other demand put in front of him before and since. If I tried to overcome his objections and push a deal, he would never go along with it. I knew it. So if I wanted to walk out of that room with a check—on fair terms—it was going to have to be *his* idea to work with me.

I took a deep breath. It was time to flip the script.

I had been working on a completely novel way of telling other people about an idea or product so that they would come up with the idea to buy without my even having to ask. It's called Inception, and it's based on the latest research in neuroscience and behavioral economics. I've uncovered a way to plant an idea deep in another person's subconscious so that they take ownership of it and propose it to me as if it were theirs.

This approach is needed because traditional sales methods get you stuck in arguments and logical stand-offs—which is where I was headed with Viktor. Inception relies on a completely new set of tools: the Status Tip-Off, the Flash Roll, Pre-Wired Ideas, Plain Vanilla, being Compelling, and the Buyer's Formula. I'll show you all of these later.

Back in Moscow, Viktor was moving fast and he wasn't giving me a chance to use any of these advanced principles. I knew what I needed to say, but he would switch the conversation to Russian at the worst possible time, and I couldn't get him to listen or understand me—he was just too good at the game. My time was about done and I'd gotten absolutely nowhere.

Try to imagine this for a second. You've spent twenty-five

minutes talking to your only prospect, and in that time you've been ignored, interrupted, misinterpreted, and told your state-of-the-art technology seems old and outdated. None of your persuasive points have found a home, and all the material you have left to deliver is no better than the stuff that's already been rejected.

The problem I was facing in that room is the same problem salespeople face in any industry: You know what decision you want the buyer to make, but the more you push in that direction, the more they dig in, slow down, and change the agenda. They want to make *their own* decision on their own timeline. Buyers buy how they want to buy, not how you want to sell.

This is why today most things are bought; they aren't sold.

I realized that Viktor had pushed me to act like an amateur salesman and I was trying too hard to pitch him on the merits of the deal. I reminded myself to stop selling and instead establish myself as an expert, because a smart buyer like Viktor would never do a fair deal with an amateur.

I was ready to create Inception but I was also nervous to try this new approach on such a powerful dealmaker. Hopefully Viktor couldn't tell how anxious I was feeling, but then I realized it didn't matter. Inception doesn't involve feelings. I steadied myself and went back to work, focusing on elevating my status and proving my expertise.

I delivered a Flash Roll—a sixty-second display of pure technical mastery designed to alleviate any doubts about your authority on a subject. When Viktor turned to his translators for help, I was ready.

"Viktor, I do not allow you to be confused about this," I said. "You're one of the best investors in the world. And I am offering a Plain Vanilla deal, nothin' fancy at all. This is easy stuff. And we are almost out of time, so for the moment, you have to accept what I'm telling you at face value."

He nodded in acceptance, and I could tell I had impressed him. By flipping the script on him, I'd taken him by surprise. "Continue, please," he said imperiously, as oligarchs generally do.

Finally, I had the chance to reveal something called a Pre-Wired Idea that I knew would act like a back door to his mind. The moment you deliver a Pre-Wired Idea, buyers suddenly understand everything they need to know about what they should do next, without you having to explain it or sell it or even say anything at all.

My time was nearly up. "Viktor, this deal is a great fit for your company," I said. "But you already know that. So let's figure out what we're going to do together. Just tell me one of these two things. First, if you don't want to work with me, just say, 'Oren, I don't want to do the deal.' It's OK—I allow you to say that to me, and we can easily part ways. Otherwise, the second option is for you to say, 'Oren, I like you and I like the deal—let's move ahead.' Those are the choices; I just need to hear one. Either one is fine with me. Just tell me which it is."

Then I waited.

It felt like a huge risk to say this, but it was no risk at all— because the alternative would be to ask for the sale, to which he would instantly reply, "Send us the information and we'll think about it." Translation: "Nyet."

The next three minutes were silent and stressful, and I finally drank the warm vodka that had been poured for me an hour earlier. The silence grew uncomfortable for Viktor, and I let him be uncomfortable. He scratched some numbers on a notepad only because he wanted to end our staring contest. No matter the pressure and risk, I was not going to chase him. He had to chase me, if only a little bit. And then, at last, the ice broke. "Can we see the data again, please?" he said politely. My method had worked. He *was* chasing me, ever so slightly. Did I jump with excitement at this moment, or pull out a bunch of charts and graphs and race to a close? No I did not. Instead, I pulled out my phone and began looking for an Uber. And while I did, I casually explained my Buyer's Formula to him, just to be helpful.

"I do these kinds of medical software deals *all* the time," I said nonchalantly, like I'm in an oligarch's office every day. "The tricky part is handling patient data." And then I explained how I would choose to invest or not invest in the deal I was offering him. "Anyway, from doing this so many times, that's just how I would look at it."

This was it—the moment it all comes down to. It was time to ask Viktor if he was "in." It was time to push him for a yes.

Except it wasn't.

With the Inception scripts, you never tell the buyer what you want them to do—you never pressure them for a yes. You let *them* tell *you* they want to buy. I looked Viktor in the eye and said, "I need to head out for another meeting across town."

And then I heard the magic words that come when you successfully take a buyer through the six steps of Inception. "I like this deal. We can work together, so thank you please, now stay," he said thoughtfully, this time in very good English.

An hour later I had a $10 million deal on fair terms, a plan to hire the needed mathematicians, and the endorsement of a Russian oligarch.

WHERE THE "OLD SCRIPT" CAME FROM

In ancient times, life was short and dangerous; survival from sunrise to sunset was not a sure thing. For much of early civilization, at least a quarter of all human males on the planet were killed every year by war, famine, tribal infighting, and things that bite, sting, inject poison, or stomp.

Everywhere you turned, there was something that could easily kill you. Moving too slow or in the wrong direction meant the difference between life and death; there was no time to second-guess yourself. Nobody else could be trusted. To survive, you needed to trust your own judgment above that of all others, no matter what, acting on your own ideas without hesitating, and resisting the influence of risky outside ideas. Anything new and foreign is untested and, therefore, not to be trusted. **The human brain is thus wired by evolution to distrust any information from the outside world and to greatly favor that which originates inside us.**

Since childhood, others have been trying to smuggle their ideas into your mind. So naturally your mental defenses have gotten *really* good. It's as if you have a small team of cognitive security guards and bouncers who are trained to keep unfamiliar and confusing ideas away.

But salespeople are well trained too. The typical sales script tries to push past this resistance by exploiting your survival instincts, or the patterns of thinking you use when you're stressed and need to move quick, without time to think. Consider these sales scripts: "I have another buyer on the line who wants it." "This is the last one we have in stock." "It's *thirty percent off!*" These statements may sound innocent enough, but they are actually carefully constructed mental manipulations designed to stress your natural decision-making system.

In the past, buyers accepted a high-pressure sales script as an unwanted but necessary part of the buying process because they genuinely needed the information that only an experienced sales rep could provide. But today, everyone can find, research, and buy anything online—so high-pressure sales scripts are not just unwelcome, they are hated.

In fact, these tactics are so outdated that even car manufacturers are abandoning them. In their studies, car companies found that the high-pressure scripts do more harm than good, often causing people to do the opposite of what you're asking, just to prove that you aren't controlling them—a phenomenon known as psychological reactance.

The way most people think of it, the act of selling is defined by psychological pressure. Salespeople always end up at this uncomfortable moment when they need to "close" and get the buyer to commit. But the buyer always responds in the same way:

- First, by pacifying the seller: *"Yes, yes, this looks terrific, you really have a great product."*
- Second, by backing away: *"I just need to look a little more closely at the numbers."*
- Finally, by deferring the decision to an unavailable third party: *"I will need to talk to my partner; he needs to approve an important decision like this."*

If you've ever tried to sell anything to anyone, you've heard all this before, and you already know this is where deals go to die. Yet most salespeople feel pretty good when they get to the end of their pitch and the buyer says, "Yes, yes, this looks terrific, I just need to look a little more closely and talk to my partner; please write up everything you mentioned in a proposal, send it over, and we will discuss it and get back to you." In fact, you shouldn't feel good at all, because that deal is as good as dead.

THE SCIENCE OF INCEPTION

If you've ever bought a product you didn't even know you wanted, or made choices that seemed a little out of character, then it's likely you've had an idea implanted in your mind.

Inception is the allegedly impossible implantation of an idea in someone's mind so that they think it's their own. It involves the ability to introduce parts of an idea to someone and create the perfect conditions for the whole idea to "surface" as if it were theirs, not yours.

You may have seen this in the movie of the same name. *Inception* is a 2010 Academy Award–winning sci-fi-action thriller written and directed by Christopher Nolan. In the film, an industrious neurological spy steals inaccessible, secret information from the mind of a rival businessman. The character's mission is to plant certain ideas within his rival's subconscious mind.

Like many good science fiction stories, the movie invented some of its own science. But it is seeded with a kernel of truth. Creating ideas for other people, however unlikely it may sound, is not only possible, it happens every day at the highest levels of business and government.

Have you ever seen a sign that reads ONE PER CUSTOMER and immediately thought, "I'm going to figure out how to get *two*"? This is a classic form of Inception. You simply forbid an action in order to encourage it, creating a kind of universal Do Not Push button that everyone wants to press. The reason? None of us want to be told what to do.

But this example is just a hint of the full power of Inception, as I'm about to show you.

Certainly I did not invent the Inception method. It was always there in plain sight. I just uncovered it and explained how it works best in business situations. After all, writers for detective shows such as *CSI* and *Law & Order* have been implanting ideas in our minds for years. Consider how watching one of these shows always leads you to a moment when you as the viewer are able to put the pieces of the crime together and figure out who did it. You might say something like "I know what's going on here! It *has* to be the cop—he stole the drugs and set the whole thing up!" This moment is predetermined, inevitable.

You feel a rush of excitement when you identify the culprit before the big reveal happens on-screen, but that was always the writers' plan. You're meant to discover the answer on your own and feel good about it. That eureka moment has been carefully planned and programmed to deliver an insight at exactly the right time. When you put the pieces together before the detectives do, you feel smart, happy, powerful, and in control (exactly the emotions needed to motivate you to buy some canned beer, frozen pizza, and extra-soft toilet tissue). And you tune in next week so you can feel that way again.

Even if you don't watch crime procedurals, you've probably experienced a moment like this, when a solution to the problem you're working on suddenly materializes in your mind. Something just clicks and you see the answer. It feels almost like divine inspiration. You don't doubt it. You don't second-guess it. You trust it, believe in it, and act on it immediately—because it was *your idea*. And we are certain about our own ideas.

We don't just find it satisfying when our brain comes up with ideas on its own, we also value those ideas more highly. If you handed someone an origami swan folded out of plain printer paper and asked the person how much they would pay for it, they might say they'd pay nothing, or just twenty-five cents. Almost never a dollar. But if instead you taught them step-by-step how to fold the same swan out of plain paper themselves, then asked them to estimate the value of the paper bird they'd just folded, you would get a much higher number. Maybe three dollars or even four. Researchers have proven this many times in multiple settings.

The same is true with an idea. Make people feel like the idea is coming *from them* and they will place more value on it, believe it more deeply, adopt it more quickly, and remember it more easily.

This book will reveal the Inception script to you. In the pages that follow, I will show you exactly how to target the part of the brain that produces the feeling of *Ding! I've got it!* When you present an idea like this, everyone who is listening will trust and believe in it because the idea will feel like it originated in the depths of their own minds.

So how do you plant an idea in someone's head in a way that makes them feel like it was theirs (especially if you're not the head writer for a long-running crime drama)? Researchers have found that Inception moments arrive suddenly, in a burst; there is no gradual buildup in the brain. We sit there, pondering all the pieces of the puzzle, and at some point, out of the blue, there is a huge spike of activity in the superior temporal gyrus, a tiny bundle of neurons on the right side of the brain, just below the temple, that's tied to the feeling of certainty we get when an idea is our own. And then, a short while later, we consciously know the answer.

When you can reliably re-create this exact sequence of events in the mind of the person you are trying to influence, you will be able to trigger Inception.

Does that sound impossible? Or like science fiction? In truth, it's neither. It starts by throwing out the old scripts. I'm going to teach you a new one. Master these six techniques and you'll never have to ask someone to do what you want again; they will come up with the idea all by themselves.

CHAPTER 2

The New Dominance Hierarchy

Who gets what, and why?

It's tempting to think you should get financial rewards in a fair way, according to your effort, sacrifice, and contribution, and while this might sound great in the gospels, *it is not how we as a species operate.* Humans operate, and have always operated, within a rigid power framework that I call the *dominance hierarchy*, **where the few who exist at the top get more of the best of everything, and those at the bottom get the scraps.**

For the last million years it was nearly impossible to change your social position in society without an army behind you, because status was based purely on physical strength. Life was a simple system where the biggest, toughest, most aggressive members of a social group would get anything and everything they wanted until they were eventually challenged and killed by an up-and-comer in a never-ending cycle of life and death.

Something changed around the first millennium. As human tribes got bigger and more complex it was no longer possible to challenge everyone to fight in order to establish your place in the social layer cake. A new dominance hierarchy emerged in which social status surpassed physical size as the means to influence others.

But we never truly mastered this new dominance hierarchy. **Even today, improving your social ranking rarely happens easily, quickly, or even at all because your ranking is one of the most difficult things to change unless you have been trained to do so.** Social mobility for most people is fixed at birth. Unless you are very lucky and get picked out of a fast-food restaurant while wearing a chicken suit like Brad Pitt or can throw a 99-mile-per-hour fastball like Max Scherzer to earn $200 million, social mobility is limited.

While those on top ultimately fall, and those on the bottom eventually rise, this typically occurs across a span of several generations. The hard truth is that you inherit your underlying social ranking from your parents the same way you inherit your height. **In other words, your birth is your fate unless you master the tools that will allow you to change your position in the social layer cake.** The problem is that most people have misunderstood the process of how to do this.

But it can be done.

After spending many years studying the science of power and dominance, my team and I have discovered a way for you to match status and power with anyone, in any business or social situation. And it takes only about thirty seconds to pull off when you understand how it works. In order to explain the process, and why it is so effective, I need to introduce you to Ötzi the Iceman.

Ötzi excited the scientific community when he was found frozen in the Italian Alps in 1991 in near-perfect condition. Finally, archaeologists would be able to study the daily routines and social structures of a 70,000-year-old man. An analysis of Ötzi's stomach's contents revealed that his last meal was ibex (a horrible-tasting kind of deer) and poison fern.

Ötzi didn't have a very good last couple of days, and it's doubtful he had many good days at all during his short nomadic life. His toes were mangled from years of frostbite, half his teeth were gone, parasitic worm eggs filled his intestines, and he was partially blind from repeated doses of fern toxin. But it wasn't the poison that killed him—it was an arrow in the back of his head from some locals whose territory he walked into. That area must have been "locals only."

The day he was killed, Ötzi either had the wrong kind of tattoos or was wearing the wrong color of clothing or didn't have the right amulet on his arm. What scientists have discovered after studying Ötzi's remains, and the remains of others like him, is that early humans relied on visual cues to determine social status and tribal affiliation. As tribes got bigger and the social layer cake expanded, we had to start responding to external cues of power such as uniforms, tattoos, clothing, family crests, and titles. It soon became second nature for us to recognize and act on these indicators of position and power.

Today, a mix of subtle visual and verbal cues help you instantly recognize the social status of people around you. The way you dress, the precise words you use in conversation, the tone of your voice, and your behavior in specific situations will all telegraph your status within a group or society at large.

When you learn to recognize and control these words and symbols, you can change your position in the social layer cake at will. You can enter a completely unfamiliar social group in just a few seconds and create enormous influence in the process. During the past few years I have worked with the high-status ultra-rich on some very large deals, and I've seen the power of simple cues to rapidly create wealth or leave behind missed opportunities. In the process, I've mastered a new set of tools that will allow you to change your position in the dominance hierarchy by simply uttering a few sentences. That's how I closed one of the craziest deals of my career.

IN SEARCH OF $25 MILLION

I was speeding down Rexford Drive in Los Angeles, past heirloom hedges and giant wrought-iron gates that concealed some of the most legendary real estate in Beverly Hills. During the next two hours I was going to have one shot to make a $25 million deal, which was not an ideal situation because this deal looked manageable when I started, but now nothing about it was going my way and at this point there was only one man who could help.

John King is a very wealthy but very off-the-grid loner with no attachments who was unreachable by phone and popped up only for the occasional hit-and-run media appearance. Think of him as the billionaire business version of Jason Bourne. Since 1999 his website had only two words, "coming soon." His receptionist was an answering machine. Nobody in my Rolodex could connect us, either. For two weeks I'd been searching for him, because this was the man I needed to pitch my deal to. It's not that he was avoiding me; he just didn't know I existed and hadn't been around to hear my offer. But that's something I knew how to fix. Let me explain:

My business model is pretty simple. People hire me to do three basic things:

1. Get meetings with wealthy investors.
2. Pitch them an irresistible offer.
3. Close the deal and get the money.

I charge a lot for this kind of work, so nobody ever hands me the easy jobs, and over time I've become the patron saint of tough deals. If no one else can get it done, *Just give it to Oren*, people would say.

My client on this deal was a successful solar company with plans to buy a large plot of land in Arizona and build a lucrative energy farm. I had promised to find and deliver $25 million, which should have been a manageable task. Except it wasn't. One problem had led to another and every investor I'd lined up had evaporated before their wire transfer came through. It was starting to feel like this deal was cursed.

With time running out, I now had no choice but to focus on a single investor who could snap up the whole deal. That put me on a collision course with John King, one of the top energy investors in the world. For a guy like John, this deal was just the right size for a quick yes. A guy on his level could do it with a handshake and two sheets of paper, if he loved it. But, of course, he wasn't going to be easy to persuade because he wasn't easy to find.

With the clock ticking and my repeated attempts to get in touch with John coming up short, I was close to losing my commission while making quite a few people angry. If you're in sales or have ever had a big deal lined up, you've probably been at this point before, where your hopes of success are dwindling and suddenly you're open to new suggestions or doing some things that seem a little out of character. That's how I decided to attend the unusual sounding Altitude Series conference, which was part music festival and part business meet-up, and not my normal cup of tea. But a reliable source had told me John was possibly going to attend, and that was all I knew. The situation didn't sound very promising, but I was down to try anything.

While typical business conferences are usually held downtown at a large hotel near the convention center, the address for the Altitude Series took me up Benedict Canyon to a mansion in the North Beverly Hills. The founders of Altitude were rule breakers. After all, they had once asked me to help them buy an entire mountain ski resort, which I did, and which is how I knew them in the first place and was able to get an invitation. As I pulled up to the gate, I started to enter a different and unfamiliar world, as you'll see in a moment.

Cars were parked up and down the street, but according to my invitation I had "VIP access" and "on-site valet parking," so I hit the call button, announced myself, and the enormous gate creaked open. I pulled my car onto the circular drive and up to the private residence, which was the size of a country club.

As I pulled to a stop by the fountain in the center of the cobblestone driveway, a young valet stepped toward my window with his hand outstretched for the keys. The car I was driving might not look like much to you, but my red 1971 Alfa Romeo Sprint GT is an enthusiast special and I spent three years restoring it. Nobody touches it but me. I rolled down the window to tell the valet what I always tell valets: I want to park it myself, no offense, happy to tip you, just point me to an open spot.

"Oh yeah, I figured you'd want to park it yourself," the kid said, talking fast.

But what he said next, I wasn't expecting at all. "I just was curious whether you had the dual-Weber carb-kit, because it sounds like you're running a set of four-valve, flat-top, *forged pistons*." That immediately caught my attention. He continued, "I bought a 1969 Sprint last year and had Simon at Alfaholics blueprint the motor with that same setup. . . . "

Those forty-two words acted like a secret code to let me know this kid was on a completely different and higher level of the social layer cake than I'd initially thought. In about eight seconds I went from thinking, *This random college kid is going to dent my car*, to *This fine young man can hook me up with Simon at Alfaholics!* Clearly he was an enthusiast at my level, and probably even higher.

Without a second thought I tossed my keys to the kid, along with fifty bucks. He smiled and slid into the driver's seat of my prized Alfa, as I walked toward the garden entrance. "I've got a safe spot on the other side," he shouted. Perfect. I never looked back.

THE CONFERENCE

Think for a moment about the last business conference you attended. Exciting? Probably not. Most conferences are tiresome industry events you want to leave as soon as the main speaker has wrapped up, but I knew Altitude was different and special the second I walked in because to the left and right, the famous and nearly famous packed the entire backyard and house. Live musicians played in small alcoves. Celebrities mingled with other beautiful people at cozy bar stations. Small stages had been erected at the outside perimeter of the garden for speakers to hold forth on various topics like climate solutions, artificial intelligence, energy, and space. I'd come here to talk to John King, but I was getting distracted by all these casual conversations between some of my favorite movie stars and musicians around every corner.

Hungry, I grabbed a tempura roll from a bar off to the side. Not more than twenty seconds later, a guy who looked a lot like John King passed right in front of me, then angled off to the right and into the dense crowd. I darted after him, catching another glimpse as he slipped into the main house, which was packed with people. It was King for sure. Though his net worth was rumored to be $2 billion, there was no mistaking his signature outfit: 501 jeans and Rush concert T-shirt.

I dashed into the foyer, but King was gone just as fast as he'd come, and I was left scanning a sea of smiling faces. Where did he go? I realized then, it wasn't going to be easy to find a man who didn't want to be found.

I kicked myself as I thought about the drawer of concert T's I had back home and was wishing I'd brought one of my own Rush shirts. It would have been an easy icebreaker for the eventual moment I would come face to face with John. But it's critical to keep in mind that shallow similarities and shared interests do not deliver the powerful kind of status alignment you need to create influence, persuasion, and inception.

ACHIEVING STATUS ALIGNMENT

If you want to understand the power of status alignment, a good place to start is at the opposite, or *status mis-alignment*. For example, have you ever put in a call to customer service (maybe for a credit card charge you didn't recognize) and found yourself on the phone with an agent who doesn't have enough power to solve your problem? As your frustration grows, you insist, once again, that you be transferred to a manager. Nothing else will do.

Sure, you could just keep talking to the helpful-sounding agent who is patiently listening to your situation, earnestly trying to solve your problem. But you won't stay on with them long, because the moment you realize this person is not going to be able to help you, they become irrelevant. Even if they're trying to make helpful suggestions, dutifully explaining the company's policy, you tune them out completely, staying on the line for only one reason: to get bumped up to a manager who has some real juice and can quickly fix your problem.

This is a very specific kind of failure where a person of high status and one of low status try to work together, and it doesn't work at all. It's the feeling you experience whenever you're talking to someone who is in the wrong part of the dominance hierarchy, either too low or too high. At first, it's frustrating. The more you talk to them, the better you come to understand they will not be able to help you. As frustration mounts, you reach a point where you tune them out and look instead for someone at the right part of the food chain to connect with.

That frustrated feeling you experience on the phone with a customer service representative who can't help you is the same feeling someone else gets about you when they feel you're not on their level and you don't understand their issues.

You cannot get the full attention of a decision maker to listen to your idea if they think you're on a different level of the dominance hierarchy than they are. When you're going to press someone toward an important decision, you first need to be sure he or she feels they are in the right place at the right time with the right person. To accomplish this, you must create Status Alignment.

Status Alignment comes when you're in front of a decision maker and you have perfectly raised or lowered your own status to match the decision maker's view of himself. Armed with this understanding of how the dominance hierarchy works, I make sure to carefully staff each of my business deals with a talent stack that any other dealmaker can recognize and easily plug into. My talent stack usually looks like this, starting at the top and in order of importance:

1. Me (the dealmaker)
2. Financial Officer
3. Marketing Officer
4. Sr. Analyst
5. Legal
6. Client Relations
7. Jr. Accountant
8. Assistant

Eight people for one deal. Why stack up all this headcount and expense? Because when the deal is underway, it's essential to get my team members to match up correctly with the other side's team. I need my analyst to talk to their analyst, my lawyer to talk to their lawyer, and my finance person to talk to their finance person, leaving me to talk directly to their CEO or decision maker— as equals. These are the correct matchups. It has to be this way because "bad matchups" create an out-of-whack dominance hierarchy where the wrong people are covering one another, assuring the deal will go sideways and eventually blow up.

The idea of bad matchups couldn't be more true in business than it is in sports, military, or other professions. So it's useful to think about this in context of making a deal or orchestrating any high-stakes sale. Even if you're a salesperson or a one-man shop, you still will benefit from having a working team of virtual assistant, technical person, and an accountant. Not to impress others. Not to showboat or hotdog. The simple purpose is to lighten your workload and most importantly to create alignment.

To maintain Status Alignment, put yourself in the lead position, keep yourself scarce, and only do things that are consistent with your status on the team and as the one in charge. The easiest and best way to influence a decision maker is when you are in Status Alignment.

Here's another example to help make the point. Imagine you're visiting your brother in the hospital. You don't have to know the nurse's name and life story in order to understand her position in the dominance hierarchy, because she has a uniform and badge to signify it. When she asks you to step outside the room so that a medical procedure can happen, you obey. Humans have no trouble accepting that something symbolic, such as the uniform and ID card, can signify position and power in the hierarchy.

But could a nurse ever tell you what to think or what you should or shouldn't believe in? In other words, would you change your attitude about something important because a nurse ordered you to? Probably not. Only someone on your level, such as a close coworker or friend, can truly and deeply influence you in a way the nurse never can.

This is the difference between obedience and influence.

When the nurse orders you to head to the waiting room, you do it—you're obedient. When a judge tells you to report for community service, you do as you're told. In these situations it's easy to see how the other person is above you in the dominance hierarchy.

Accordingly, you follow their orders. But neither the nurse nor the judge has really influenced you or changed your beliefs in any meaningful way.

Influence, and particularly Inception, is most effective when the person you are speaking to feels like he or she is on the same level of the hierarchy as you. **This is where Inception is strongest and works the best.** Before you can implant an idea in someone else's mind, you need to create a feeling of Status Alignment. That's what happened with the valet at the front gate of Altitude. In less than thirty seconds I realized he wasn't an average parking attendant; he was a car enthusiast and at my level in the sports car world. I immediately felt he could be trusted. It's a simple example, but perfectly illustrates the *feeling* of Status Alignment. And that's exactly what I was about to do to one of the biggest real estate investors on the planet.

But first I had to find him.

IS ANYONE IN CHARGE HERE?

As "cool" and "hip" and "unique" as the vibe was at the Altitude Series, it was still a business conference, and conferences are never great places for getting deals done because there are so many distractions going on from minute to minute. You barely have anyone's attention for thirty seconds before they are pulled away to the next most important conversation. But there is one huge advantage to conferences: Your target is always easy to find because everyone wears a brightly colored name tag highlighting their name, industry, and position.

I quickly ran into a problem at Altitude, however: There were no name tags, there was no information booth, and nobody seemed to be in charge. Now, I was standing stiffly, like a big confused dummy looking for "Hello My Name Is" tags or colored badges on lanyards or just a shirt that said STAFF. But there was nothing even close. I was starting to get frustrated because John had to be nearby—after all, I'd just seen him a few minutes earlier.

I stood on a small ledge to get above the crowd, scanning for John a little too conspicuously by moving my head back and forth like a broken radar dish. I was soon drawing attention from some other conference goers. An attractive woman said, "You look so tense." Her companion said, "Relax . . . Altitude is a special place to meet new friends, find empowerment, and connect with yourself."

I didn't want to connect with myself. I only wanted to connect with John King.

The women locked their arms with mine and swung me firmly in the wrong direction toward a bar in the corner of a patio. They insisted I have a drink, so I asked the bartender what beers she was serving. "Heineken, Budweiser, Corona," she said. "What'll you have?" Well, that was definitely not the greatest selection. "C'mon," I said, leaning in closer. *"Did I walk into a bar mitzvah by mistake?"*

"Yeah, tell me about it," she said, rolling her eyes. "Not my call."

I've found that if you accuse a bartender of serving "bar mitzvah beer" you'll get one of two reactions. About half will stare at you blankly; they have no idea what you're talking about. In this case your bartender is a college kid picking up some extra change by working a conference. But the other half will roll their eyes and say, "Yeah, tell me about it . . . this beer selection was not my call." These are real bartenders who know their stuff.

As my bartender rolled her eyes, I said to her, "I'm always looking for a low-sediment hop in a skunked mash, high final gravity with long head retention. Last event I went to they had a few bottles of Tactical Nuclear Penguin. Probably the last few bottles on earth."

"No way!" The bartender's pupils dilated.

Tactical Nuclear Penguin, or TNP, sounds like a joke, but it's one of the top ten beverage brands in the world and a holy grail of the beverage industry—in other words, the rarest and hardest-to-find beer on the planet and completely unforgettable by name and reputation. At 64 proof, TNP is the strongest beer ever made, and just 500 bottles were produced in 2009. Today, each bottle goes for more than $1,000 on the black market.

Now the bartender's eyes were locked with mine. "How was it?" she asked.

"Truthfully," I replied, "it tastes like shit. But that's not the point. I had to honor the fact they even had it!" Then I asked conspiratorially, "Hey, you're not holding one back there are you?"

There was a moment of silence in which the bartender looked at me in a new way—then she broke into a laugh almost as if I really existed to her now for the first time. She leaned in toward me, as if to reveal a new conspiracy. I had achieved Status Alignment with a Los Angeles bartender at a busy event, an almost impossible task under any conditions.

"I'll tell you what," she whispered. "I've got something for you in the kitchen, be right back."

A minute later I had in my hands a bottle of Founders Breakfast Stout, a truly fantastic drink, just as my new friends pulled me away toward an alcove where a group was gathering.

We sat on some logs on the grass in a mini-amphitheater as a guitarist took the stage to play with a small celebrity trio. This guy was artful. He pulled off the most insane crosspick I'd ever heard—which is the fine art of using a tortoiseshell pick to create a distinctive and beautiful cascading musical effect. He down-picked from the bottom string, ascended, playing three notes at a time, and then immediately up-picked. I had to admit, the guy was beyond good. But what I was really focused on was what he was wearing: a Rush T-shirt. There was no doubt: I had found my Guitar Hero and his name was John King.

THE SCIENCE OF THE STATUS TIP-OFF

If you were a gorilla, there would be only one way for you to achieve Status Alignment with a fellow member of your species. You would have to be roughly the same size and age and physical condition. That's because in the old dominance hierarchy your position was determined entirely by who could physically dominate who.

The new dominance hierarchy doesn't work this way. Humans respond to status indicators so small they are nearly imperceptible to outsiders. In fact, we quickly and easily respond to invisible status indicators that are entirely verbal, like "I'm agent Smith, LAPD." Those four words will make you pay attention quickly.

After noticing this phenomenon, I've spent years investigating it with my private research team, and we have discovered the most efficient way to achieve Status Alignment at the start of any conversation or negotiation with any other person. I've gradually honed this approach, using it in many large deals across various industries. It works perfectly every time when you follow a specific pattern using a three-sentence phrase called a Status Tip-Off.

Think about high-stakes situations in movies—for example, a first meeting between two spies in Moscow's Red Square, exchanging stolen missile blueprints. One spy will ask a question of the other that nobody else could possibly know the answer to—for example, "Do you know the way to the Blind Monk Tavern?" when no such tavern exists. The right answer is like a password.

The same strategy is also used in body-swap stories in TV or film, when characters become trapped in completely unrecognizable bodies. For instance, in the original Star Trek series, episode 24, Dr. Janice Lester, who was once Kirk's lover, traps the captain into a life-entity transfer, allowing her to take over his body and leave him trapped in her body. Janice (in Kirk's body) becomes captain of the ship, leaving Kirk (in Janice's body) locked in sick bay trying to convince Spock that he's actually Kirk. What does he say to prove to Spock that he is the real Kirk?

"Spock," he says, "when I was caught in the interspace of the Tholian sector, you risked your life and the Enterprise to get me back. That's when the Vians of Minara demanded that we let Bones die," if you remember. This line is a Tip-Off. When Spock hears it, he immediately realizes that this is the real Kirk. This Tip-Off—like the directions to the Blind Monk Tavern—functions just like a police officer's badge, a firefighter's uniform, a doctor's stethoscope, or a gangster's distinctive tattoos. If you're a leader in that group, you can recognize another leader immediately. And you'll listen to them, trust them, and choose to work with them over someone who is not in your group.

In the early days of the Italian Mafia, bosses in the Mazzarella clan in Naples wore distinctive rings in the shape of a lion's head. They were ruthless and universally feared, and so when you saw a lion's head ring coming your way, it was best to step aside. Mafia informer Nicola Cangiano once told prosecutors how to identify members of the Sagaria clan: "They all wear Samsonite shoes and cashmere socks." Best to stay out of their way, too.

Most of us don't have a secret code or distinctive outfit to signal to others whether they should approach or stay clear. But we can easily use verbal tip-offs. Whether you're a barista or an account executive at a bank, you have a certain domain of expertise that won't mean a thing to outsiders but that insiders will understand immediately. It's easy to think of a statement that would allow someone else to assess whether you're in their group and at their level. These are Status Tip-Offs, or pieces of information that, in the eyes of others in the know, immediately cement your status as an in-group member. A Status Tip-Off is like a password muttered through a slit in the door that signals you are OK to be let inside.

When you bump into someone who grew up in your hometown, they don't need to say much for you to feel an instant sense of connection. "Remember when Eskimo Joe's burned down back in '97?" is usually enough for you to be fully convinced that the two of you have tons in common.

But keep in mind that if all you have in common is Eskimo Joes or that you both are fans of the Dallas Cowboys or have visited the same small town in Switzerland, you may have a pleasant connection but you do not have the kind of alignment you need to do a business deal.

In business, you need a specific type of Status Tip-Off, one that reveals a certain series of ideas that could only be known by an in-group member. Once you have the right Tip-Off, the right doors will open for you. The best way to find a Status Tip-Off is to interview three people who are the same level as the person you are trying to influence. What would they say to each other, to catch up on each other's business, peer-to-peer?

Memorize your Tip-Off and find an opportunity to deliver it to a decision maker. Then sit back and watch doors start to spring open for you—because you will have just separated yourself from all the other people trying to get this person's attention. When this is complete, you will be in ideal Status Alignment with your target, ready to take the next step toward Inception.

Over the years my team and I have learned to use the three key elements that make up a successful Tip-Off:

1. Use Specific Industry Lingo
2. Describe a Recent Action You Have Taken
3. Mention a Real Situation Everyone in the Industry Cares About

Back in North Beverly Hills, watching the man in the Rush T-shirt cross-picking with his tortoiseshell, I was in deep thought as I pondered how to deliver the right Status Tip-Off to John King.

A STATUS TIP-OFF WORTH $25 MILLION

I had my target in sight, but while he strummed onstage in front of dozens of adoring listeners, he was clearly unapproachable. I settled in and tried to have a pleasant evening among the wealthy elite; I had no choice in the matter.

At the end of the music set, row after row of admirers and attendees descended upon John and the other celebrity musicians. In this "feel-good moment," common sense told me there was a near-zero chance of getting John's attention to talk about a business deal.

But I was confident that I had the one thing that will get anybody's attention in any situation: the Status Tip-Off.

Earlier in the day I'd gotten into Status Alignment with the valet and then the bartender, but it was going to be a big step-up to do the same with the elusive billionaire. I still knew my deal was something he'd want to invest in, but I also knew now was clearly not the time to go into details. If I started telling him all about the deal without first aligning myself as an equal, he'd categorize me as an annoying outsider and I would never get his full attention again. So as the crowd thinned, I stood off to the side talking to another guest. Finally, it was time. John was practically alone. As he leaned down to pack up his instrument, I knew I wouldn't get a better chance than this to introduce the deal.

"Hey, John King, right?" I said casually, keeping my hands at my side. "Don't think we've formally met but I helped you guys close the ski mountain deal for Altitude." That gave us something in common, and a reason for John to pay attention for another few seconds.

Now I was set up to use the Status Tip-Off formula. First, I would have to use industry-specific lingo. Second, I needed to discuss a respected action I was taking within the industry. Third, I needed to refer to an open issue everyone in the industry was talking about.

"I'm betting that Grid Connected Micro Inverters are the next billion-dollar market. Anyway, that's why I helped State Bill 350 get through the senate, to get rid of the caps on meter credits. I think it will be good for all of us when waiver on Assembly Bill 802 gets through in September. . . . Money is going to start pouring into the market."

John looked up. Those 68 words had snagged his interest.

"I'm headed to Arizona tomorrow to lock-up a new solar deal," I continued. "You probably saw the presentation already? Not as exciting as buying a whole mountain but pretty good for the investors, it pays a 12 percent coupon during the first twelve months. Anyway, maybe we can chat sometime."

I chose those words carefully, so John could see we were at the same level of status, authority, and power. People in the same position of the dominance hierarchy are drawn to each other magnetically.

"Wait," John said, "I didn't catch your name."

Bingo. That was the sign the Status Tip-Off had worked. John turned toward me with new interest and alertness, our status now perfect in alignment.

"Oren Klaff," I replied. "Aren't you on the board here? We probably know ten people in common. Anyway, good to meet in person."

"Yes," he said, sounding unsure but interested. "Your name does sound familiar. What's this solar deal?"

Boom. Deal junkies always want to know what their peers are working on and hate missing out. I paused and looked at him carefully. Most salespeople would have taken this as an invitation to pitch their whole deal, uncomfortably trapping their prospect in an awkward social situation for twenty minutes or more. But I knew his question only meant one thing: "I'm a little busy right now, so I'll give you a few seconds to show me you're someone worth taking a call with." John and I shared some contact information—and he later that week invested big in my solar deal.

Everything was stacked against me that day, but I was able to get the full attention of my last-ditch investor because I worked hard delivering a compelling Status Tip-Off, and securing Status Alignment. These techniques take practice, but they can be mastered by anyone. Next, we'll go further. I'll show you how to become a complete, undisputed expert in the mind of any listener in about ninety seconds.

CHAPTER 3

Creating Certainty

I always knew Project Windbreak was going to be a tough deal because The Swiss had a reputation for being tough dealmakers, and yet we flew straight to Switzerland and booked ourselves a meeting with a group of the most tightly wound, risk-averse investment bankers in Geneva in hopes of convincing them to invest in my client, a six-foot-four-inch, four-hundred-pound Steelers fan from Columbus, Ohio, named Billy whose only knowledge of local Swiss culture came from drinking Swiss Miss hot chocolate, which was the sister brand of his other favorite food, Slim Jim (both produced by the Conagra company of Chicago). So no, he did not "fit in" here.

Yet here we were, Geneva, Switzerland, about as far from Columbus as you can get, ready to sell Billy's cutting-edge cybersecurity technology, codename Project Windbreak.

We had come to Geneva at my suggestion for one reason only: a full one-third of the world's private money is stockpiled here in 350 separate "family offices," as they are called.

Our plan was simple (and probably naive). We would meet with a venerated boutique Swiss bank on their own turf and convince them to invest in our company, take a place on the board of directors, and then use their prestigious brand name and reputation to reassure other, larger European institutions that it was safe to roll the dice on us and Windbreak.

I was staying at the Four Seasons des Bergues, situated on the banks of the Rhône River, in the heart of the city, with a view of the perpetually snowcapped French Alps. It was the only place in town where I wouldn't starve to death—I need more than just the Swiss staple foods of bread, cheese, and alcohol to survive when I'm on the road.

Billy, however, is a lot less picky. His favorite meal, he cheerfully explained to me on the flight over, consists of pepperoni bread, a deep-fried corned beef hash and sauerkraut sandwich, and something he called the Buckeye dog, the details of which I begged him not to share with me. Suffice it to say, Billy would give five stars to just about anything on a plate as long as there was a lot of it—which there never was in Geneva unless you bought three of the same thing. And three of anything in Geneva will cost you a lot more than you want to pay, no matter what it is.

As a result, Billy was staying down the road at the Hotel President Wilson, which served the largest all-you-can-eat breakfast in town. But that wasn't the only reason Billy picked the Wilson. It's well known in cybersecurity circles that back in 2016 during a summit at the UN, the Hotel President Wilson's computer servers were infected by a spy virus and wound up recording some highly sensitive conversations between world leaders. After this incident, the place became legendary among cybersecurity geeks— and Billy was definitely one of those. Billy had been working at a top-ranked university to develop the next generation of voice ID systems for financial institutions and other top-secret entities such as the FBI, DOD, and NSA. Billy's latest offering was designed specifically for banking centers, where hundreds of millions of dollars were moved with a single phone call. He had created a way to not only ensure the caller was who they said they were, but to measure the stress level in the voice to determine the emotional circumstances surrounding the transaction and guarantee it was being made voluntarily. That may not matter when you're transferring a hundred dollars to your kid's college debit card, but when $1 million is leaving your account headed directly to some random company in the Cayman Islands, verification is something you care about—a lot.

Our first meeting was with one of the oldest, most prestigious banks in Geneva, that had practically invented the concept of Swiss banking and the reputation for Swiss certainty. They were exactly who we needed as partners and investors.

I had pulled up to the President Wilson at precisely seven-thirty, which left us thirty minutes to get to our meeting at the bank headquarters on the Boulevard Helvétique, check in, and be announced by eight a.m. on the dot, a full hour before I usually wake up.

It was now 7:41 and still no sign of Billy. I was getting ready to go inside and pull him away from the breakfast table when he came rushing out the front doors balancing three croissants in one hand and two different-sized mugs of hot chocolate in the other. He climbed in the car and handed me one of the mugs.

"It's Nestlé," he said, as if that was something rare and exotic, then added with glee, "It's complimentary!"

"You think you have enough food rations to survive the fifteen-minute ride?" I asked Billy, who stopped for a moment and looked like he wasn't sure he did. Before he could rush back to the buffet for another few thousand calories, I told the driver to get on the gas—we had some time to make up.

Fortunately, the United Nations wasn't in session, so traffic was light. In less than fifteen minutes we pulled onto a circular gravel driveway and into a parking lot where rows of luxury sedans and a few Ferraris waited patiently for their owners to emerge. A valet opened Billy's door and he climbed out with his hot chocolate (the croissants were long gone).

"You cannot take that in," I said firmly. The valet nodded in agreement. "I'll take that for you, sir," he said in an impeccable English accent.

We entered the lobby, which echoed our footsteps and turned our conversation into whispers the way cathedrals do. It was massive, with flagstone and steel and a wall of glass through which I

could see acres of bucolic Swiss countryside with the Alps loom-
ing in the distance, just beyond the morning fog that rose daily off
Lake Geneva and melted away like pixie dust by noon.

"Can I get you a cappuccino?" the receptionist asked us. Billy,
of course, nodded. I was just glad he didn't ask for four of them—
and a doughnut.

A man I presumed to be our host, Monsieur Lustenberger, materialized in the lobby, made his way over to us, and, nodding
crisply, offered his hand. "Monsieur Klaff, Monsieur Campbell,
thank you so much for coming. Right this way, please."

We followed as Lustenberger led us to an exquisite executive
conference room where three men who looked just like him stood
up at attention as we approached the table. They were all thin and
tall and taciturn, in suits so flawless and skillfully tailored you
couldn't even imagine where you would find such clothing—and
even if you could, it still would never look right on you. You had to
be a Swiss banker to do a suit like that justice.

"You have come a very long way to visit us," said Monsieur
Philippe, as we were introduced. "How can we be of service?"

Of course, by offering to "be of service," these men were really
asking us in the characteristically Swiss way: Why are you and
Professor Pepperoni Pie over here shopping your investment opportunity in Geneva when you should be shopping closer to home,
like Palo Alto or San Jose? Did you strike out there and come to
us thinking we wouldn't know about it because we're nestled in
the Alps?

Just as I had suspected, this was going to require a bit of script flipping or this meeting would quickly be over. What little these men knew about our company was enough to pique their interest and schedule this meeting—barely—but they were clearly far from sold. It was our move, and we had to make it count. When you're in a situation like this, being met right off the bat with skepticism—albeit very polite Swiss skepticism—you have to play your cards exactly right.

Billy was about to speak; the next words out of his mouth would either make us a $10 million deal or get us run out of there. Luckily, we'd been rehearsing this moment for weeks, and he knew exactly what to say. It was time for a Status Tip-Off. But he'd need more than just Status Alignment to instill certainty in these bankers. Billy needed something else. He was going to have to say something that would cement his position as an absolute authority in his field (cybersecurity) in the mind of every person in the room.

FILLING THE CERTAINTY GAP

Building a dream home is something many people look forward to for years. But the moment you're ready to make it happen, the first thing you'll realize—before you can get anyone to do a lick of work—is the number of people who start asking you to write checks. Very large checks.

To start with, you're going to need an architect, and it's going to take a few bucks up front to get a good one. The architect wants you to pay immediately, and sends you an invoice for something like fifty thousand dollars, *due upon receipt.* In other words, show me the money.

Pay the whole thing up front? *Are you crazy? I could get ripped off!*

This is the classic transactional puzzle: In a given deal, how much financial risk should you accept? How much risk should you expect the other party to accept?

To sort this out, you talk to the architect about payment terms and come to the following arrangement: You'll pay 50 percent of the total in advance and 50 percent when the plans are delivered. Yes, he can harm you by taking your advance payment and not completing the work as agreed. But you can also harm him by not paying the final bill. So "half now, half later" is a very useful form of a "mutually assured destruction."

Does this work? Absolutely.

In the United States, this simple formula is responsible for at least $1 trillion of deals each year: 50 percent in advance and 50 percent upon receipt.

What's happening below the surface is that you and the architect are both seeking enough certainty to go ahead with the deal. You each want the sense of control—that you're not at the mercy of the other party.

Our ancient ancestors didn't have to deal with this problem because before the invention of money, they relied on a system of *equal barter.* An ancient man from Mesopotamia might have traded a hammer tool to another man from Babylon for a stone pot. These men would *not* have trusted each other—but it didn't matter. There was always complete certainty in bartering situations because each party immediately got the thing he wanted. In direct barter, you're never left waiting and hoping the other party will follow through on their end of the deal.

But in today's world, when you're selling an idea, a company, or a service to be performed in the future, the buyer can no longer hold it in their hand and have it immediately when the deal is done. Today, almost every transaction has inherent uncertainty, which makes us uncomfortable because our brains are wired to expect the type of total certainty our species experienced for a million years in equal barter.

Whenever your mind desires 100 percent certainty about a deal but your gut says it's got a 50 percent chance to work out, you're mentally experiencing a Certainty Gap. The larger this gap gets, the more you will start to feel psychological anxiety and even physical distress—causing you to back away from the deal.

Every decision we face, every purchase we make, and every agreement we enter is a function of great uncertainty.

When a buyer says, "I need to think about it," at the end of a presentation (a common response), it means they don't have enough certainty and confidence to move forward. Sure, what you've promised sounds good, but what if it doesn't work out as you say? How can the buyer be sure?

The goal of every sales presentation is to reduce the Certainty Gap in the buyer's mind—improving the chance of getting to yes.

THE LINE BETWEEN TOO LITTLE
AND TOO MUCH INFORMATION

The standard method for closing the Certainty Gap is to provide the buyer with more information. For example, we could inform him about some of our recent accomplishments, list twenty other firms we've worked with, talk at length about our features, things like that.

This is the classic sales script: *Give us the money and we will deliver as promised.* Look at all these customer logos—and here's a testimonial, two awards, and a thousand "likes" on social media.

Instilling certainty is different from creating Status Alignment. With Alignment, your goal is to show the buyer you're similar to them and make them instantly feel like you "get" them—whether you're talking to a coal miner or a Fortune 500 CEO. To instill certainty, on the other hand, you need to prove that you are a complete, absolute, undisputed authority in your field. So, in Billy's case, his Status Tip-Off would have to prove to the room full of Swiss bankers that he's one of them—an experienced and well-connected banking professional. Then, he would need to prove his bona fides as a cybersecurity expert . . . all within two minutes.

GETTING TO STATUS ALIGNMENT
WITH SWISS SKEPTICS

I had spent weeks preparing Billy for this precise moment. What he said in the next couple of minutes would make or break all our efforts. He needed to prove to these men that even though he might look different, eat different foods, and dress differently (Go Buckeyes!), he still belonged in this room; he was a critical part of the banking industry. He needed to create Status Alignment. To start, it was time for a Status Tip-Off.

He adjusted in his chair and said, "Excuse me." All eyes turned to Billy. "I like these offices you have here," he said with a smile. "Beyond impressive. An almost perfect Victorian restoration."

The Swiss nodded appreciatively at the compliment.

Billy continued, "Then again, when I take a closer look"—his eyes squinted slowly—"it's not really Victorian, is it? Take this room, for instance, overlooking the gardens. The design of the room is all about proportion and balance, with sash windows, stucco cornices, the six-paneled door. This is older than Victorian, right? It's way older. There's a kind of symmetry and grandness . . . hmmm—oh, of course, now I have it. These construction elements were really part of the Georgian era, where wealth and influence were on more conspicuous display."

He crossed the room as he spoke and gazed out the large windows along the southern wall of the room, overlooking miles of lush countryside, dramatically pausing for ten seconds.

"I especially admire these windows. With eight large panes there's more glass in here than modern building codes allow, and I'm sure you know, in the Georgian period, the number of windows in a house denoted how wealthy a family was, because there was a heavy window tax at the time to help fund the war effort.

"These windows . . . they're a signature for you, right? High ceilings, grand views, they add to the feeling of being among the 'financial elite' when you're in this room. It makes me feel like I'm in an iconic Swiss bank—don't take this the wrong way either; it's just terrific, I love it!

"But the windows, they're a problem too, aren't they? Physical security here is obviously impossible . . . anyone with a two-dollar crowbar can waltz right in."

Then Billy struck a dead serious tone, and stared directly at Philippe as he continued. "Guys, there's no way in hell you're ISO 2700 cyber compliant under G7 banking regulations, so you can't trade directly with any financial exchanges, right? NASDAQ, Börse, hell, even SIX Swiss probably won't take any of your buy-sell activity."

I had no idea where this was all headed, but I was loving it. By starting with the architecture and history, he was showing he understood these men culturally. Now, with a shift into a discussion of banking transactions, he was aligning his status on a technical and business level.

"You have no real ability to secure this—your *main office*—so you can't have any high-speed servers on-site, right? They'd be totally exposed!" Billy was not really asking—he knew. "So no servers here. . . . Aha, you're renting co-location racks at remote sites?

That's a real pain—I estimate your trade times are, what, a hundred milliseconds per cycle?" He chuckled. "A hundred milliseconds is a joke. In Akron, we're making trades in less than two milliseconds.

"Look, don't take this the wrong way. You guys are terrific; I love this grand architecture, the gravel driveway stacked with Ferraris, and the European traditions—and this cappuccino right here is one of the best ever—but let's get real with each other. When someone in this office puts up an order to buy or sell stock, you have to send it to a remote trading desk two hundred miles from here to process at a millisecond cycle time. You guys must be getting *killed* with that lag time. I mean, you might as well be placing trade orders from the North Pole.

"Listen, if you're interested, I could take a look at your setup and recommend a security work-around. You could definitely get your trade times down to inside of ten milliseconds without much work. I bet we can get you into the three-to-five-millisecond range in about a month. But anyway, just a few thoughts; I know we're here today to talk about my company and our software . . ."

Holy crap, that was unbelievable. Billy had just laid down a flawless Status Tip-Off. He had nailed a major pain point for these guys: They were two hundred miles from the nearest banking exchange and were operating without a banking compliance rating— that's like trying to get into an exclusive New York City nightclub with a note from your mom. They were surely the slowest trader in the region, and in banking, slow means last in line. Not a good way to run a bank.

Philippe stroked his chin thoughtfully. "Yes, this is true," he admitted. "The trading lag costs us millions every year but we cannot bear to move to another location. It is a tradition that we bank here, in Geneva. This building is a part of our legacy."

"I can see why," I said, jumping into the conversation. "It's beautiful. Trust me—if anyone can help, it's Billy. But let's shift gears for a minute. Let me tell you about the latest technology this guy has been developing."

The four men all nodded, leaning eagerly toward us. I could immediately tell from their body language that Billy had achieved Status Alignment. They were interested and viewed him as a peer. We'd cleared the first hurdle.

But now things were going to get more difficult. It was time to explain the deal and how Billy's complicated technology worked.

I would do this using a Pre-Wired Idea (more on that in the next chapter). But before I could get to any of that, we had to provide the bankers with a sense of complete confidence that Billy and his product were worthy of a $10 million investment, and that he would use the money properly. We had to instill certainty.

When you ask someone to give you $10 million, it's stressful for all involved; because the stakes are high and a no really means no. You need the buyer to feel certain you're a good bet. The problem Billy and I were about to face is that when the "buyer" is a team of the most calculating and risk-averse men on the planet, and you are an ex–Ohio State linebacker turned computer security guy from Akron, this level of certainty isn't naturally occurring. You have to create it.

Thankfully, my team and I have found a solution to this problem. Billy was about to fill in the Certainty Gap using a very specific type of script called a Flash Roll.

THE FLASH ROLL

In the film *My Cousin Vinny* there's a classic scene in which the prosecutor, played by Lane Smith, is questioning a witness, played by Marisa Tomei, who is on the stand as an auto mechanics expert for the defendant. Smith's character is trying to prove that Tomei's character, Mona Lisa Vito, an attractive Brooklynite with heavy makeup, big hair, and a too-tight dress, just isn't qualified to comment on the details of the case. He sarcastically asks her, "Can you tell me, what would the correct ignition timing be on a 1955 Bel Air Chevrolet with a 327 cubic-inch engine and a four barrel carburetor?"

"It's impossible to answer. . . . Nobody could answer that question!" she replies.

"Your Honor," the lawyer declares triumphantly, "I move to disqualify Miss Vito as an expert witness." The judge seems to agree. After all, with the hairdo and tight dress, she looks like she knows nothing about auto mechanics. Everyone in the courtroom is thinking the same thing: *What could this woman possibly know about cars?*

But then Tomei delivers one of the most iconic speeches in film history. In about fifteen seconds, she establishes herself as an absolute automotive authority and completely changes the way everyone in the room sees her. Even the opposing lawyer is impressed and has nothing more to ask.

How did she instill so much certainty in so little time?

"It is a trick question," she said, talking a mile a minute. "'Cause Chevy didn't make a 327 in fifty-five. The 327 didn't come out till sixty-two. And it wasn't offered in the Bel Air with the four-barrel carb till sixty-four. However, in 1964 the correct ignition timing would be four degrees before top dead center."

As she finishes, a stunned silence hangs over the courtroom. Only an expert in automotive mechanics could have made that assessment and explained it so thoroughly, rapidly, and matter-of-factly.

"Well . . . uh . . . she's acceptable, Your Honor," Smith says meekly, admitting her testimony before sitting back down.

This is a classic *Flash Roll*—a linguistic fireworks display of pure technical mastery over a complex subject. A Flash Roll is specially designed so that no matter how skeptical your listeners are when you start talking, by the end they'll be convinced you're a total expert and you know your industry and your craft cold—down to the finest detail. The Flash Roll should take just sixty to ninety seconds to deliver—that's about 250 words.

Have you ever taken a mountain bike to a repair shop? To your mind, all you know is the brakes don't brake and the shifter doesn't shift. The mechanic—that's the guy with tattoos of flames, flowers, playing cards, and sea serpents covering both arms and a slick hipster mustache—takes one look and says,

"Look here, you've got a worn control arm at the gear insert point where the guard plate connects to the head sprocket and you have too much plate pressure so the trailing edge is catching the gear cable every time the spoke set rotates toward the center hub . . ."

"Stop," you say, fully convinced this hipster bike guru is a technical master in your precise problem. You happily hand over the bike and leave with complete certainty that the fix will be done correctly, to the highest standards. This makes the seven-hundred-dollar repair bill easier to swallow.

Without knowing it, the bike shop repair guy just delivered an impeccable Flash Roll.

A good Flash Roll must locate a problem; it should take a point of view and it should arrive at a deductive conclusion about how to solve a problem. You need a Flash Roll with a clear beginning, middle, and end.

What you want to create is an action sequence delivered in highly technical language, which does something special to establish you as an expert. There are no creative thoughts in a Flash Roll. There are no statements such as "then I noticed" or "and that made me start to wonder" or "I started to think." You are not explaining your philosophy, you are not throwing out a few ideas for discussion, or passionately talking about your business or product. In fact, a Flash Roll is told dispassionately, with no emotional content or display. It must be completely stripped of all editorial, emotional, and extraneous details; it is literally just a list of technical actions that can be taken to solve a very difficult problem. Without ego or pride or even charisma, it should explain exactly what you did to solve a specific problem and then what the outcome was. And, of course, what makes the Flash Roll fun to perform is that you are going to purposely use dense, technical jargon that most people will tell you to avoid using. For about ninety seconds you're flipping the script.

An important and helpful step is to memorize your Flash Roll so you can deliver it at double your usual rate of speech. Think of it this way: As written, a Flash Roll is about 250 words. Your average rate of speech is probably 125 words per minute. So in order to get through the whole thing in about 60 seconds you'll need to speed things up quite a bit. When you're delivering a well-written Flash Roll at this pace, the buyer has the sense that you're simply describing something you've done or dealt with a hundred times before. Especially when you make such a decisive conclusion on such a specific problem so matter-of-factly. The fast pace with the technical detail and the finite conclusion will make it obvious that you are for real.

You start a Flash Roll by making the problem seem simple, routine, or trivial—to you, it's something so basic, you hardly think about it. For example, consider a time you showed your doctor a rash that wouldn't go away. "Oh, yeah," the doctor said, "we deal with these all the time. Had a guy in last week with a plant-induced contact dermatitis . . . had to give him furosemide to reduce the edema, and do a quick photorefractive laser pass; it was touch and go, but finally got him out of critical with an endovascular aortic aneurysm repair. . . . But looking at yours, it doesn't look half as bad as that—you probably just got a meningococcal septicemia and we can knock it out with a course of epinephrine and quick Z-Pak." And even though you don't have a clear idea what she's talking about, you instantly relax. *Good*, you think, *this doctor knows what she's doing. I'm in good hands here.*

To write your Flash Roll, describe the problem being faced, your assessment of it, your proposed solution, and the economics (how long it would take and what the results would be, or were the last time you did it). Freely use technical terms, writing exactly the way you talk to the technical people in your business when you're one-on-one with them. Recall the mechanic at the bike shop explaining what is wrong with your bike. Or think about the doctor who looks at the rash and says, "It's nummular dermatitis. We'll treat it with oral cyclosporine, topical corticosteroids, and ultraviolet light therapy for a week and you'll be good as new."

Doctors have a flawless Flash Roll. They may not call it that, but their job depends upon their ability to instill a sense of certainty in patients that the treatment they are proposing will work for them—even while at the same time saying, "There's no guarantee this will work."

The manner in which you deliver the Flash Roll is of the utmost importance. **You absolutely cannot be seeking validation or opinion of the buyer.** You are the expert, not he. This Flash Roll assessment shouldn't come across as something you are proud of. Instead, it should seem like it's mundane and uninteresting to you—not a big deal at all; like if I asked you about it in a few hours you might forget you even said it.

To end the Flash Roll, you can just shrug and say something like, "Anyway, based on what I'm seeing here, that's what I would do." Then leave it all behind and move on to the next part of the presentation.

In one deal I was involved with, Heather, an incredibly smart sales executive wasn't getting a good hit rate on her sales calls with clients. Heather was extremely knowledgeable about her industry and how her software worked, but no sales were coming in. So they sent me out to talk to her.

As soon as I saw her I immediately understood what the problem was. Heather had cropped blond hair, a rock climber's physique, and dressed smartly for the corporate world. And she was trying to sell software to logging mills, a completely male-dominated industry where everyone drives pickup trucks, has a chainsaw or two in the back, and in October every year puts enough frozen elk in the fridge to make it through winter. Most sawmills haven't been modernized and suffer from operating inefficiencies, which Heather's software is designed to fix, but first she had to convince a bunch of male sawmill executives to see her as an expert, to trust her recommendations, and most important, to be certain her software would fix their problems.

I worked with her to write a Flash Roll that would get the mills' executives believing in her abilities, and told her to practice it as if she were learning a movie script. Yes, it was a business presentation, but I suggested she treat it more like a theatrical performance—after all, it was just for 60 seconds. At her next meeting, she landed the sale and over the years became a top executive in the industry.

Here's what I wrote for her, word for word:

Last week I was at one of your competitors' sawmills, where I saw that a new 50-megawatt heat-recovery unit had been installed on a black-liquor recovery boiler with a 2,000 tons per day load setting. They spent $50,000 to install it, because of a 200-watt surge-induced power shutdown, but they didn't think to regulate the motor brush speed, so that Johnson X4 heat-recovery unit needed to be removed and rebuilt with ceramic 228-needle bearings. The problem turned out to be a 75-psi pressure drop at the weld joint where the air fans couldn't handle the volume, shutting down and jamming all the NOS valves. We came in to install and override the processor and adjust the electronic pressure valves, which worked perfectly first time out, and they've increased pump production 200 percent, saving over $10,000 a month on downtime.

Boom. That's only 138 words. About one minute of speaking at normal speed—thirty seconds when done at double the normal pace, as I instructed Heather to do.

Even though I wrote Heather's Flash Roll, I didn't fully understand it. Most people would not. Arguably, the experienced sawmill executives—the very people who are supposed to understand this stuff—might not get it 100 percent. The goal, of course, is not to deliver this kind of information for understanding and comprehension, but to demonstrate your technical mastery in such a way that you create certainty about your authority and expertise.

Your customers don't actually want to know the details that are in your head. If you gave them the full benefit of your industry knowledge, it would be overwhelming and time consuming, moving further from a sale rather than closer. So you create a mini-performance that you own, by delivering the Flash Roll with focus and impact. Of course, most of us aren't professional performers (this is why you keep a short time limit). But for this brief display of mastery of the details, we can all learn our Flash Roll script. **It's critical to do this correctly because the buyer wants the comfort and confidence that you are an absolute expert,** that you can get down in the weeds if needed, and the Flash Roll shows them that you can do it, without question.

In Geneva, Billy was going to deliver a Flash Roll we'd spent weeks crafting. But first, he had to lay the foundation.

WARMING UP

"Gentlemen," Billy began, "the top ten highest-paying jobs in data security today are . . ."

[long pause for dramatic effect]

". . . are all completely bootleg, criminal, and illegal. Let me quickly tell you about the top three moneymakers in the data industry:

1. Stealing data and reselling it on the dark web
2. Encrypting data and ransoming companies to decrypt it
3. Hacking bank accounts and making fraudulent transfers

"And the good ol' days of the amateur account hacking ransomer are gone," Billy continued. "We now have well-funded nation-states like North Korea, and traffickers like the Sinaloa Cartel who are playing the bank fraud game.

"When you hear the word *hacker*, what's the first thing that comes to mind? A twentysomething alone in a basement, wearing a black hoodie, staring at a laptop. In the old days, sure, you wouldn't be far off the mark. Now we're defending banks from professional criminals: the Russian Business Network, the Carbanak group, Cosa Nostra, Yakuza, and the Sinaloa drug cartel. These groups are stealing data and hacking accounts at two petabytes a day, worth $10 million each, with almost zero cost. This criminal activity is invisible to most corporations, until it's way too late, so hardly anyone will pay the high cost of installing better safety systems."

Billy was starting the pitch by providing context for what was happening in the industry—the specific undercover forces that most people didn't know much about—further cementing his status as a cybersecurity guru.

"Today," he continued, "the hackers are well-funded, difficult to identify, and very industrious because the black market for stolen data pays so well. Incredibly well, in fact. It's a world of high revenue and high profit. A criminal data operation can go all the way from idea in the morning to operations in the afternoon and then to a million in profits by the end of the day."

I had written this section of the presentation around the Pre-Wired Idea "Winter Is Coming" (more on this in the next chapter), painting a picture for the bankers of just how bad things were getting. We needed to show them that the world they lived in was becoming unacceptably dangerous.

"Hackers will try *all day every day* to access your customers' accounts and their money," Billy said, staying on script. "That's why you ask each customer so many questions when they call, right? But the customer is annoyed by so many questions—birth date, PIN, last transaction, et cetera—and the process takes an average of five minutes and seventeen seconds to ask them all the identifying questions. You and your customers currently accept this inconvenience as a necessary evil to keep the transaction 'secure.' But customers sure don't like it."

Some of the bankers were nodding their heads. This was definitely hitting home.

"What if it wasn't necessary at all?" Billy continued. "Our system identifies the caller using their voice in less than five seconds. We're never wrong. We do this using our own unique voice identification algorithm and by comparing what they are saying to every known piece of information about them on the internet. If there is any question they are not the person they say they are, we flag it immediately. It's an unbeatable system."

Because this topic was so relevant to the bankers' world, they became visibly emotional as Billy spoke, shifting in their seats.

Their body language revealed that Billy's words were hitting a nerve. But I knew we were still a distance from the finish line. We still had to convince them that Billy was capable of spearheading this company—and was worthy of the $10 million we were asking for.

As if on cue, Philippe spoke up. "Tell us, Billy, if we provide you ten million dollars, how will you spend it?"

Now, Billy was tech smart. He was food smart. He knew literature, seventeenth-century architecture, college football rankings, and, of course, cybersecurity. But he wasn't the greatest at international diplomacy. He jumped in without giving a thought to where we were (Geneva), whom we were asking for money (Swiss citizens), and where we were going to haul their money off to (Akron, Ohio).

He rushed to explain. "First, we're going to build a new data center in Akron. Then, we're going to hire six or seven engineers from Carnegie Mellon University in Pittsburgh. And we're going to partner with NASDAQ. And our first big customer is going to be Bank of America. We might park a couple employees at their headquarters in Charlotte, North Carolina . . . just for a while to monitor implementation."

In other words, all that money would leave Switzerland, be spent in the United States, and only benefit Americans. He might as well have said we were going to spend it all on new outfits for the Dallas Cowboys Cheerleaders. This was *not* what they wanted to hear.

"Why should we give this American company our investment when there is no benefit to the Swiss?" Philippe asked, starting to frown. "The board of directors would never approve it."

There was a long silence as the body language in the room

cooled off. Pens were put down, chairs were pushed back, coffee cups clanged back in their saucers. It was like one of those scenes in the movies when a character does something embarrassing and the music comes to a screeching halt.

We were in trouble. I jumped in.

"Guys, let me interrupt here for a moment because the best part of our plan is next—we're going to open an office in Zurich." Their heads nodded approvingly. Whew. "And we're going to hire five Swiss engineers and open an internship at Swiss Federal Institutes of Technology." More vigorous nodding. "And, of course, we would expect to hold the annual board meeting right here in this office—if you would agree, of course." A murmur of approval.

This explanation diplomatically solved the geopolitical turf war Billy had started. But now we had a new problem: Billy's slip-up had broken the spell we'd cast over the Swiss investors. I could see them sliding back into their natural state of skepticism. They started firing questions at us.

"What do the projections look like?"

"Do you have a CFO?"

"How many additional rounds of finance will be required? Who will buy us when we want to sell the company off?"

Rapid-fire, penetrating questions like this are always bad news. With his statement, Billy had unintentionally triggered the buyers' brains to become aware of the risks we were offering. Now these bankers were trying to gather more information to close their Certainty Gap. The problem is, we didn't want to answer, because answering technical questions is an inefficient way to close the Certainty Gap and rarely works with sophisticated buyers.

We needed to figure out a way to flip the script. To do so, Billy had been practicing an incredible Flash Roll, and this was the right moment to launch it.

I took a gamble and interrupted the interrogation. "Gentlemen," I said, and pointed to one of the men at the table, "one question at a time, please. Professor Schumacher, what were you asking?"

"You obviously know data security," said Schumacher, "but our banking industry has special requirements; these may be difficult for you to learn in such a short amount of time."

I breathed a silent sigh of relief. It was the perfect question to set Billy loose with the Flash Roll. Billy rushed in to answer again, but now he was in the right domain—cybersecurity, not international diplomacy; this was an area where he was an expert. And this time he was about to deliver a well-rehearsed masterpiece of a speech, not just something he was making up off the cuff.

These guys were about to see a very different side of Billy Cambell.

Billy grabbed a fat strawberry from the platter in the center of the table and dipped it into the bowl of sugar by the teapot, and the whole thing disappeared into his mouth. He was fueling up for his Flash Roll, or as I sometimes call it, a drum solo. He knew this was his chance to make the deal happen.

A $10 MILLION FLASH ROLL

"Unlike retail or manufacturing," Billy said, swallowing the straw-berry in a single bite but not slurring a word, *"banking IT security controls are required by the EURO2 to be multilayered and to meet Unified Threat Management on the server side, which re-quires firewalling, intrusion detection, and anti-malware. We use Palo Alto Networks' PA-5000 to cover these gaps. But that leaves software-based security holes on user-side devices, so all banking exchanges will audit your end point protection to go beyond the host-based network side and do an AJAX pass root on the user's device in external environments that do not provide network-based security controls like Level 3 Boundary Protection. Of course, we still need data encryption rest cycles at two hundred milliseconds, which goes way beyond end point encryption to wide net cloud storage. That's why the ten largest banks are using mul-tifactor cryptographic tokens and biometrics at the current ISO2026 standards, a system that we designed and sold them."*

Whoa. What just happened?

This went way beyond Status Alignment and hit every credibil-ity button a banker has.

Although Billy was speaking in a very matter-of-fact tone, he was also speaking at twice his normal pace, so this was an impres-sive amount of technical detail in a short period of time. It was a drum solo of sorts, a wonderfully produced Flash Roll, for bankers only, and when he wrapped up, there was no question that Billy was a technical master in the domain of banking security—precisely the kind this bank needed to solve their problems. He didn't *tell* them how he "knew" the industry or list his extensive credentials. He *showed* them. It was an easy script for him, scrolling through technical details, software vendors, the tech stack, and security implementation. After this speech, there was little question in anyone's mind that Billy was the only man for the job. They thought to themselves, "He is the one to protect us all."

"Well, thank you, gentlemen," said Lustenberger a few minutes later, after we'd finished the rest of our pitch and turned over full autonomy to the bankers (a technique I reveal in chapter six). "We'll talk it over and get back to you in a couple of days. Are you in Geneva long?"

"We're leaving on Friday and need to know by then," I said matter-of-factly.

The very next morning we got the call from Philippe. The bank came in with the $10 million investment we'd wanted. Project Windbreak was a success. Billy's Flash Roll had turned the tides at a critical moment and left the questioning bankers with a sense of complete certainty about our experience, depth, and know-how.

We went out in search of a restaurant to celebrate and ordered three of everything, which was just about the right amount.

CHAPTER 4

Using Pre-Wired Ideas

Since my first book came out, we've had to keep the office doors locked to prevent the large number of visitors, walk-ins, and occasional crazies. Accordingly, I was surprised to see an elderly rabbi shuffle into my personal office at ten o'clock on a Monday morning. His venerable beard framed two rosy cheeks, his eyes looked like windows to a different century. He was sporting a black suit and the kind of large leather briefcase my grandfather probably carried back in Lithuania.

I stared at the rabbi and he stared back at me in an awkward silence. Then his face erupted into a huge smile as he pulled a carefully folded piece of paper out of his breast pocket and held it out to me. I did not take it.

"You see?" he asked, as if I was supposed to know. It was a

newspaper clipping announcing the launch of a biotech fund by a major venture capital firm. They had $200 million to spend and the rabbi wanted some of it.

"I need to meet with New Icon Capital right away," he said, "and get twenty-two million." He sat down across from me, opened his briefcase, and started pulling out papers slowly and methodically, stacking them on my desk.

Oh man. Some days all the stuff that comes my way is overwhelming. Today, this guy needs $22 million, tomorrow that guy needs $30 million, and then some other guy needs $50 million . . . there's no end to it.

I excused myself from the room to ask my assistant, Amy, what the rabbi was doing in my office, why he was unpacking his briefcase, and bluntly, how we were going to get him out of there as quickly as possible.

Amy had been through all of this before. Nobody was supposed to get through without an appointment. "He's on *your* calendar," she told me with a shrug. "You accepted the invite."

Now, I'm not the kind of person who checks my calendar multiple times a day, but I'm sure I would have noticed "Old Guy wants $22 million" was scheduled first thing on a Monday. I checked my phone calendar and, oops, there it was: 10 a.m., Silicon Valley Mentor Program.

Amy rolled her eyes. "You're his *mentor*," she said.

I glanced back through the open door of my office at the seventy-year-old man who was still carefully withdrawing papers from his bottomless briefcase and organizing them on my desk, seemingly in his own little world. I was his mentor? No, I don't think so.

But Amy was right. A few weeks earlier, I had volunteered for an entrepreneurial mentorship organization. It's an obligatory Silicon Valley tradition in which successful executives get paired up with a mentee who is just starting out in the business world. There are a couple of reasons why it's nearly impossible to get out of being a mentor. Not only is it the decent thing to do (and it really doesn't take much time), but more so, a cabal of lawyers, banks, and accounting firms basically require you to do it. The unwritten rule is, "If you want to get access to our money, you help our people out."

Here's how these mentorship deals are supposed to work:

- You get paired up with a twentysomething wunderkind who is creating some kind of change-the-world technology.
- You meet the kid for coffee, and listen intently while he shows you a demo.
- Most of the time the demo stalls out, or shuts down, and a colorful little circle starts spinning.
- You listen to a heartfelt speech about changing the world.
- Next, you dutifully make some calls to get them a few investor meetings.
- And of course, once they meet a partner or investor, you never hear from them again. Favor done. Case closed.

The entire process is supposed to take no more than a few hours, cumulatively. These mentees are supposed to be young, tech savvy, self-motivated, and . . . completely broke. You buy them a cortado and an almond croissant, listen carefully and try to help, and eventually they will go away. I was prepared for all that. But I had not signed up for this guy.

"Look, sir," I said, grabbing a few of his papers and stacking them back up, "I'm really not an expert in biotech. I think Simon at Biocom would be a much better fit." The rabbi pushed one of the documents he'd laid out on my desk an inch closer to me. It was a signed contract with Humana, a $300 billion company. That got my attention. I flipped to the next document in the stack. Another signed contract with Pfizer. The next document—another contract, this one with Merck. And there was yet another one with Johnson & Johnson.

"These are sort of interesting," I said, quickly adding up some of the numbers in my head, while trying to remain impassive. "You have over nine hundred million dollars' worth of contracts here."

"One point seven billion, actually," said the old man, blinking repeatedly. I glanced at the name on the bottom of every contract. His name was B. Rosenberg, the most rabbinical-sounding name in the world. Only this was no rabbi. Within a few seconds I had pulled up his Wikipedia page. Professor emeritus in biochemistry. Runner-up for national laureate in recombinant human genetics. Recently awarded an international fellowship in molecular medicine. An international ranking in developmental biology. And twenty other similar awards and honors, each one better than the next. It appeared that he had bounced around the early stage bio-tech startup world for a while, until a friend of mine, Bob Morgan at a Silicon Valley bank, decided he needed a real adviser and then referred him to me.

Wow. My very first mentee had walked in with $1.7 billion in signed contracts. Maybe I should volunteer for stuff more often. After a bit more digging, I learned that a key technology he needed to satisfy these contracts, called BioSequence, was up for sale—and he was first in line to buy it. This is what he wanted the money for. The purchase would let Professor Rosenberg cash in on the contracts, establish his company as the global leader in the genet-ics industry, and cement his stronghold on the market for genetic tests worldwide.

The problem was that he was a bit difficult to understand, had a two-hour-long story about his company and its plans, and looked like he might drop dead of natural causes before these compli-cated plans could be put in motion. There's no way he would be able to get the money on his own.

"Oren, you will get this meeting for me that I need very much?" he asked me then, and looked up at me with ancient, wise eyes. I wanted to help Methuselah here, but I had to level with the guy.

"There's no way New Icon is going to give you twenty-two mil-lion dollars to buy BioSequence," I said. His brow furrowed and his eyes filled with the sadness of the ages, and he blinked a lot. "But," I said, and he immediately brightened. "I'm willing to bet they'll give it to me." He looked relieved, but you could see his mind working, like a mental abacus adding up my piece of the action, and finally realizing that I would be very expensive. But he understood that without my help the New Icon money was out of reach. And he also knew that without the New Icon money and the BioSequence technology, those fancy contracts of his were almost worthless.

Two weeks later, Professor Rosenberg and I were walking up the steps to the inner sanctum of New Icon Capital Partners in downtown San Francisco. I'd managed to get a meeting through a contact named Jim, whom I'd worked with on another deal a few years back. This wasn't an easy meeting to get, for anybody. Their schedule was packed and my request had come out of nowhere.

"Better late than never," Jim said, sticking his large hand out and welcoming us into New Icon's massive reception area. Huh? I glanced at my watch. We were early, not late. This was exactly the kind of upside-down thinking you have to deal with in Silicon Valley where early was late, small was big, money was everywhere, yet impossible to get when you needed it most.

Jim had an imposing frame, a strong, confident face, and a crushing handshake. You knew from the second you met him he was in charge of things. Yet, he also seemed fair, a man who didn't price his words cheaply. He was impressive. And I was impressed he'd gotten us the meeting so fast. I owed him big-time.

"Let's head to the conference room. The investment committee is ready for your presentation now." Jim punched a keypad and a glass door whooshed open. Jim stepped through quickly, leaving Professor Rosenberg and me scrambling to keep up. The door slid shut automatically behind us, and just like that, the two of us were inside the top-secret world of New Icon.

We followed Jim through what seemed like a mile of glass hallway. Every entrepreneur dreams of passing through these hallowed halls, because a "yes" from New Icon means your chances of becoming a huge business success go up a hundredfold. We were walking into the financial stratosphere, our footsteps echoing down the same corridors that had greeted the founders of companies such as Pandora, Ancestry.com, Casper mattresses, Postmates, Bleacher Report—all of whom were now billionaires. We walked past two thirtysomethings whom I recognized from the front pages of the *Wall Street Journal*, each worth over $1 billion. Today we were in the midst of people who could buy the New York Jets with a check.

There was no question about it. This was serious business, and I'd spent the past two weeks translating Professor Rosenberg's obtuse and highly technical presentation into a simple pitch that investors would quickly understand and buy into. I glanced at Rosenberg, who seemed overwhelmed by the spectacle around him. I had to admit, I was feeling the pressure myself. After all, the stakes couldn't possibly have been higher. It would be known around the world in an instant if New Icon said no. Our deal would become too toxic to touch. Today, right now, we had one bite at the apple, with no second chances. I needed to calm him down—he looked so nervous he might pass out or drop dead before we got our shot at the $22 million.

"Sometimes the best thing you can do is not think, not create scenarios, not imagine, not obsess. Just breathe, and have faith that everything will work out for the best," I whispered to him. "If anything goes wrong, think, 'We'll turn lemons into lemonade.'"

"Lemons?" said Jim, who did not miss a trick. "Life has never given me lemons. It has given me stress issues, a love of alcohol and a short temper," he said, and for some reason he looked right at me.

"That didn't help," I told him, pointing at Rosenberg.

We heard only the echo of our own footsteps as we passed through on our way to the executive floor. The glass hallways gave way to a maze of cubicles. Everywhere we looked, young men and women were trading stocks across five time zones, looking for the slightest edge and chance to make a few million. We heard four loud beeps and a ding that meant $10 million had been scored with one tap of the enter key. Along the way we were joined by an analyst who asked if I'd like a cup of Panda Dung Tea, which, he informed me, is an artisanal brew cultivated in the mountains of Ya'an, Sichuan, and fertilized with the excrement of wild pandas under the direction of celibate monks and sells for twenty thousand dollars per pound.

"Can I get a Diet Coke?" I asked. "How much for a pound of that?"

"That's a Nicholas Schöffer," the analyst told me helpfully a moment later, gesturing toward a sculpture at the base of the stairs. It was a simple hunk of half-polished metal that cost twenty trillion dollars. "Did you happen to see the unveiling of his Chronos

XVII?" he continued. "Massive steel, forty-nine light projectors, and sixty-five movable disks that create a ballet of light and movement. It was a true happening."

"Wow, no, I was out of town, but I was super bummed to miss it," I said.

No question about it, this place was a money circus . . . and we were about to meet the ring master, the legendary Grant Goodman. Grant and his partner, Ross Fogelsong, founded New Icon Capital Partners back in 1989 with a small bit of money they'd pooled together. The two of them proceeded to make one savvy deal after the next, steadily growing in size and influence. Today, they run one of the most successful and widely respected venture capital funds in Silicon Valley.

"Grant's in no mood for your personal brand of humor today, Oren," Jim said to me under his breath as we neared the entrance to the central conference room. "Just stay on topic, and stick to the plan." I punched Jim lightly on the shoulder, as if to say, "No worries, bud, I got this."

"Don't do that," Jim said.

A moment later, he ushered us into a large room with a perfect view of the San Francisco Bay.

In the center of the room was a large table. It was the size of a dozen air hockey tables. Professor Rosenberg and I found ourselves seated in front of about fifteen New Icon analysts grouped around the far end of the table. They were mostly young men wearing khakis and t-shirts with logos from companies I'd never heard of, like switcheroo.net. I did the math and realized this one-hour meeting represented some very expensive man-hours for the firm. "Good," I thought. "They may not know who we are, but at least they're taking the deal seriously."

The New Icon team is the best and the brightest that the entire world has to offer. These guys are valedictorians all the way back to kindergarten, with master's degrees in computer science from Stanford, MBAs from Harvard, and for fun, a BA in ancient Greek philosophy from Yale. And most of them had not yet broken thirty.

"Here is Oren Klaff to tell you more about Gennacode," I heard a voice saying. Someone was dimming the lights and all eyes were turning toward me. It was time to say something that would help these analysts immediately understand our company's complex technology, business model, revenue projections, and deal terms. And I'd need to instill complete confidence that Professor Rosenberg could be trusted to lead the company.

Most people at this juncture would begin to list the specific features and benefits of their technology, giving these analysts all kinds of fodder to tear apart. After all, that's what they're here for. Tearing you apart is how they earn the salaries that pay for the houses and the cars and the vacations in Cap d'Antibes. I looked briefly at Grant Goodman at the far end of the table. He didn't look too happy. What could I say to change the look of mild displeasure on the wizard's face?

It was time to hit his idea receptors and begin the process of Inception.

HOW IDEA RECEPTORS WORK

Information doesn't just magically move from the outside world into your brain. There's a process. You have to perceive something in your environment using your senses (input the data), make sense of what you are seeing (process the data), and remember it for later (save the data). And before your brain can perceive, process, and save a new idea, you need to have the right type of idea receptor waiting for that information, or it will pass through you, completely unremembered or quickly disregarded.

For instance, Nikon makes a camera called the D5. Don't be scared by the $10,000 price tag. This thing is a bargain when you consider its incredible features. The D5 is equipped with an impressive native ISO sensitivity of 30,000, an insane 400,000-cycle shutter durability, and a drool-inducing lossless 14-bit buffering capacity of 12 images per second.

Woah. If those stats don't leave you dying to get your hands on one of these then *nothing* will . . . and that's exactly why Nikon doesn't market this camera to you. If these numbers don't already mean something to you, then it'll be hard to sell you a D5. In fact, in order to sell you one, Nikon has to give you weeks of photography training first—just to get you to a level where you could even understand why these features are good. This isn't just a photography problem, it's a biology problem: If your brain doesn't have receptors for information, the information is meaningless.

Where do idea receptors come from? They must be built, and

this process takes time. The receptors needed to fully understand the technical components of the D5 can take years of photography training to build. Nikon's solution? Don't even attempt to market the D5 to anybody who doesn't already have the necessary idea receptors. Only sell these cameras to professional photographers. It's just too difficult to talk to regular consumers about this product. But what if you specifically need to influence somebody who doesn't already have receptors for the ideas you want to communicate? How do you start from scratch and get someone quickly up to speed on a technical, complex, or obscure big idea?

I've found there are a few receptors that everyone has that you can use when you don't have the time to construct your own unique receptor. These receptors come pre-wired in humans at birth. Think about slot machines, drugs, alcohol, pornography, and refined sugar. These things take advantage of preexisting brain circuitry and easily activate it. The same is true of a gripping movie, a book you can't put down, a reality show, or neighborhood gossip. The reason we feel instantly hooked is because these things take advantage of pre-wired idea receptors that exist in all our brains.

A few years back I went on a quest to identify the deepest, strongest, most ancient idea receptor in the human brain, the "godfather" of all attention-grabbing ideas. I called up a few prominent psychologists at various universities and asked them where I should start looking for this receptor and their response was surprisingly unanimous. They said I should look at three areas, in order of importance: threats, rewards, and fairness.

Over the course of thousands of generations, evolution has taught us to be constantly on the lookout for these specific types of information:

- **APPROACHING DOOM:** We automatically pay close attention to weather patterns, food shortages, political unrest, new types of weapons technology, and never-before-seen predators. It's absolutely critical to be the first to know about any kind of doomsday scenario. This is different from the threat of a lion leaping out of the bush (a deadly threat that only has one response: Run!). *Approaching doom* refers to a threat that can take you by surprise because it moves too slowly for you to see it coming. A stock market crash. A new kind of predator. A food shortage. *The first person to detect slow-moving but catastrophic threats survives; others suffer and die.* The rule? Humans always give their attention to new information about big environmental threats.

- **A BIG PAYOFF:** We are always looking for a huge reward for just a small amount of effort. Since there are always costs for adopting any kind of new behavior, we aren't going to switch to something new for a puny little reward. A reward has to be nice and big before it's really worth it for us to switch to a new behavior. The rule? Humans move quickly toward large paydays that are easy to measure and value.

- **A FAIR DEAL:** No one likes to be taken advantage of, and we are very sensitive to integrity, equality, and fairness. To make any kind of deal work, both parties should feel like they're getting a fair shake. The rule? Other humans always want to be sure *you* have skin in the game and offer a fair deal before they say yes.

Our receptors for these specific pieces of information are so deeply wired that we cannot evaluate details of an offer until the "big three" are satisfied. Buyers, therefore, come with the desire to know three things above all else:

- WHY SHOULD I CARE? (What new threats and dangers are out there?)
- WHAT'S IN IT FOR ME? (How can I get a better-than-average reward?)
- WHY YOU? (How can I trust you to give me a fair deal?)

Once you answer these questions satisfactorily, the buyer will feel like they completely "get" your deal. Only then should you provide them the detailed information you have prepared. Most presentations either don't ever answer these questions satisfactorily or they take way too long to get there. My team and I have found a simple way to get your buyers feeling like they fully understand the answers to these questions for your deal in just a few seconds. The key is to specially format the information you have so that it fits perfectly into these pre-wired idea receptors—like a key fitting a lock.

That's exactly what I was about to do in the New Icon conference room, standing in front of Grant Goodman and his crack team of boy geniuses. But first, I needed to align my status with theirs.

PITCHING NEW ICON CAPITAL PARTNERS

The first problem Professor Rosenberg and I faced in that room should be obvious by this point in the book. Most of the people in the room were forced to be here; this was not elective. There was some mild interest in our topic, but we were nobodies and easily forgettable. And Rosenberg was wearing a black suit, which nobody had seen outside a Bogart film retrospective in fifty years.

The problem: We were going to have to quickly align ourselves or we'd strike out before we ever got up to bat. The fifteen analysts in the room had seen hundreds of ideas come and go along the way. It was their job to rip apart the plan, find the flaws, and in the process kill the deal. I had to become one of them, an insider, not an outside entrepreneur trying to finesse my way in.

Consider for a moment what analysts are used to seeing:

- A charismatic and bold entrepreneur with a great story to tell
- Colorful charts and graphs that all point one way: upward
- Dramatic data projections to show how one plus one is actually three
- Reassurance that all these stratospheric projections are actually "conservative" and "easy to achieve"

That's how an entrepreneur would pitch the deal. But I wasn't pitching to a room full of entrepreneurs. I was pitching to a room full of analysts. I needed to present the deal exactly the way an analyst would. I needed to use their own insider language to tip them off to my status as one of them and as a reliable source of information.

But how would an analyst present a deal to another analyst? Well, let's start with what I know he wouldn't do.

- He wouldn't tell them it was a "really good deal"; instead he would show them. He would demonstrate the truth of his statements.
- He wouldn't present a bunch of complicated facts; instead he would summarize it all in fewer than a hundred words.
- He wouldn't waste time saying please, thank you, and "How about this weather"; he would make use of every available second.

An analyst talking to another analyst wouldn't be in selling mode at all. He would strip out all the fluff, emotion, and optimism, leaving only the cold hard facts. He would show, not tell, and that's exactly how I prepared our Status Tip-Off. But first, a critical statement to signal that I was their equal.

"Good morning, gentlemen, glad we could find time to get on each other's calendars. There's a lot to get to today, and not much time to do it, so let's begin." This was an introduction showing that we were equal in status to the investors—that our time was as

valuable as theirs, and we weren't there groveling for a deal. "I'll get to the story of Gennacode and our financial plan in a moment," I began. "But first let me catch you up to the present moment: First, I have already put our financial model through the Dodd-Frank Part 325 Stress Test [this is the equivalent of running over a child's toy fifty times with a truck to make sure it's safe to play with]. So, the 12-month revenue projections will show actual cash-to-be-collected. At the same time, I have also assumed that we hire 50 percent slower than our competition. And I've assumed we will have to pay 25 percent more for everything than they do. And I've assumed our customers will stretch their dollars and pay slow."

With these five simple statements, only about ninety words, I'd shown that we were already looking at our plan more negatively than they ever would. In other words, I had already done their work for them, ripping the numbers apart with a "stress test" and making worst-case assumptions. This negativity is not how you would talk to an entrepreneur or a marketing guy, but it's certainly how an analyst would talk to another analyst.

And it worked. Instead of rolling their eyes and starting to destroy our numbers, the New Icon analysts were leaning in, wanting to see what was behind a company that had volunteered to beat themselves up, to stress-test their own numbers with the Part 325 test, the most dreaded financial test out there. It was all very intriguing.

The classic signs of Status Alignment were now visible: more attentive body language, surprised and intrigued facial expressions, nodding of heads, setting aside of phones, dilated pupils, parted lips with hints of smiles. Next, it was time for a Flash Roll to show them we were clearheaded and well organized and could discuss critical technical details in a matter of seconds—unlike most presenters, who take hours to do this.

"Today in the U.S.," I continued, "health care is thirty percent of our eighteen-trillion-dollar economy. That's pills, potions, services, surgery, and chronic care. It's a massive market. Yet today only *one* technology is making high-margin dollars in every health-care segment: genetic testing. A genetic test is valuable to all consumers for three reasons: First, it predicts your chance of getting a serious disease, including cancer, diabetes, or heart disease. Second, it shows you how to prevent a disease that you are at risk of getting. Third, it will help you treat any disease condition you may already have. But how?

"A genetic test panel will indicate how you metabolize certain drugs, which is critical information for treating any disease or adverse health condition. Today, doctors and patients need genetic tests to make any major health-care decision. We sell a genetic test panel to large corporations and governments for about $450. Why is price point important? Because it's ten times less than anyone else. We have cut the price of genetic tests by 90 percent. What is our test specifically? A test that measures your DNA for 22,000 genetic markers, giving you information on more than 200 disease risks, drug responses, and health conditions. And the accuracy we're getting is in the .001 error range, using high-density micro-arrays, thermo compacting nano-robotics, and the new generation of pooled-library multiplexing with a proprietary enzyme-catalyzed DNA polymerization process."

I hadn't "sold" anyone yet, but I had accomplished something crucial: All the analysts relaxed in their chairs. Some had been holding up pens, ready to raise their arms a little higher, to interrupt with challenging questions. They put down those pens. They no longer needed to ask disruptive questions because my prewritten Status Tip-off and Flash Roll had caused them to feel reassured, thinking to themselves, "This is awesome—for once, I'm in the hands of a professional presenter who knows what he's doing. I'm just going to sit back, listen, and enjoy the presentation."

Next, I would give them the three pieces of pre-wired information their brains were craving.

THE 3 W'S

During a presentation, you need to convey not one but three ideas to the buyer; these are the 3 W's: Why should I care? What's in it for me? Why you? And if you don't want them to tune you out, you need to demand as little mental energy from them as possible while you explain these things. I've developed three Pre-Wired Ideas to do just that. These ideas activate the risk, reward, and fairness receptors in your listener's brain to deliver the key pieces of information a buyer needs with a sudden whoosh of insight.

Why Should I Care?

It's a simple matter to answer the first question using a Pre-Wired Idea called Winter Is Coming. This targets the threat receptor. An example of how this works is clearly seen in the story of Microsoft's big comeback. When Satya Nadella took over as Microsoft's CEO in 2014, the company relied almost exclusively on its Windows operating system for revenue. The stock price had been pretty much flat for the previous ten years and the company was seen as a has-been giant of the tech world, on its way out.

Nadella had to tell the company, all 131,000 employees, that things were about to get a whole lot worse for them if they weren't able to make the jump to cloud-based computing, and fast. He made it clear the Windows operating system was not going to keep paying the bills forever.

Winter.

Is.

Coming.

For tech giants in today's economy, things have changed. Operating systems don't make money. Instead, Search makes money. PCs are dead and everything is mobile. People don't buy software; they rent it. Everything is on the cloud. If you cannot shift to cloud computing, you freeze and die. That's what "winter" looks like for a tech giant.

Nadella took major, dramatic steps to avoid Microsoft's fast-approaching winter. First, he took an $8 billion loss to completely shut down their smartphone division. He moved Word and Excel programs to the cloud, risking another $8 billion. He spent huge portions of cash reserves building cloud computing data centers all over the world. By 2018 Microsoft's stock price had nearly tripled, and by November of that year, the company that had recently been written off as a has-been made international front-page news by passing Apple as the most valuable company on the planet.

What had motivated Microsoft and its 131,000 employees to pull this off? The tangible fear of being caught in a slow-moving but completely nuclear winter; the risk of total annihilation from the marketplace and the primal fear of being thrown into history's trash bin of has-been technology. This is the Pre-Wired Idea: Those who do not perceive, prepare, adjust, and adapt to changes in the environment are wiped out. Microsoft was able to adapt and prepare for its winter, yet this company is one of the few that did. When major changes approach slowly, most businesses are caught off-guard.

This is the Winter Is Coming narrative, and you can tell this story in any industry on any day of the week. Tell your listeners that everything they rely on to thrive today will soon be gone—and it's happening faster than they think. Provide thoughtful examples showing why the way they run their business won't work much longer. There's an early winter coming, and if they don't do anything to prepare, adjust, and adapt, they'll get wiped out. In the meantime, others who do prepare will outlive them, step into their turf, and thrive—by taking their place in the industry, as well as their customers.

How to say this, exactly? For one, I would never tell a prospect that I have a better product than the one they are currently using, or that I have a new and better idea. I would just say that the industry as we know it is transforming, and I know how to operate successfully in this new playing field. As I like to say, the person who knows what will happen next and in the future is always the most important person in the room.

What's in It for Me?

The easiest way to fully activate the "what's in it for me" reward receptor is to use the idea of 2X: that something important to them will double in size, productivity, efficiency, competitiveness, output, or just plain happiness and satisfaction. Here's how it works.

First, take a moment to consider how often you buy a new cell phone. Manufacturers release new models at least once a year. But do you personally upgrade your phone that often? Most don't, because the models that just came out are only slightly better than the one you bought last year. The average consumer waits a few years to buy a new cell phone, until they feel switching to a newer model will truly be a substantial upgrade. The same is true with cars. You don't trade in your car as soon as the new model comes out every year, because the new model is at best 10 percent better than last year's model. It's an improvement but just isn't worth the high cost of switching.

So how much of an improvement does a new product have to be over the old one for most buyers to feel like it's worth the cost of switching? My team and I have observed that people don't feel ready for a new car until the latest model is at least twice as good as the one they're currently driving, miles and all. If you're into smartphone cameras, you'll probably wait until the new phones hold a lot more photos and deliver something like twice the photo quality in terms of resolution, sharpness, and accuracy.

Double is a magic number. Anything less than that is often not enough to activate and immediately satisfy your buyer's reward receptor. You need to make it obvious your buyer is going to get at least twice the results in some area with your idea, product, or service—hence 2X. Conversely, show them that they will reach the same result but cut their expenses in half.

We've found that even an 80 percent improvement, while impressive, doesn't really push people to snap to attention, hold still, and listen carefully. People are so busy with their lives that switching over to your new great way of doing things is a bit of a hassle. So you need to find some areas where your deal is providing double the value, twice the speed, or half the cost of what they have now. It can even be something subjective, such as "You'll feel twice as good about yourself" or "Cut the hassle in half," as long as it follows the 2X formula.

Why You?

The last thing the buyer needs to know about your deal is "why you?" How can they be sure you are still going to be around after the deal is closed to handle any problems? In my world, investors want to know that the CEO of the company is not going to give up and quit when things get hard—and things always get hard. It's not enough to say you are credible, hardworking, and trustworthy. What proof do you offer of this? What evidence can you provide to show that you'll stick with it, work hard, stay focused, and follow through?

Evolutionary psychologists Leda Cosmides and John Tooby have confirmed in their research that we all come pre-wired with a fairness receptor—in essence, a cheater-detection system. We are constantly on the lookout for cheaters and we love to see them punished—we literally crave the experience of fairness. But how do you show someone that you won't try to game the system or quit the job early?

Here's the answer we discovered: The only way for a buyer to be 100 percent sure that you aren't a lightweight who is going to bail when things start to get difficult is to see how heavily you are invested in a successful outcome. Your personal investment proves you have as much to lose as they do. It shows this is not a one-sided deal, and you both have skin in the game. The easiest way to help your audience to arrive at this feeling is to activate the fairness receptor using a Skin in the Game script, a quick story that shows how you are financially, physically, or contractually committed to this opportunity—maybe even more than you are asking them to be. In other words, you've made real sacrifices and paid the price to be here. It's not simply that you'll feel bad or look bad if something goes wrong; it's that you'll lose something important to you. The deal you're presenting is set up so that your money, time, and professional reputation are all on the line. There has to be some evidence that you won't stop when you're tired—you stop when you're done.

When you get good at providing this Pre-Wired Idea of Skin in the Game, it's an easy matter to combine these three concepts into a single script that includes all the elements necessary to activate the threat, reward, and fairness receptors in your buyer's mind. In summary:

- The Winter Is Coming script answers "Why should I care?"
- The 2X script answers "What's in it for me?"
- The Skin in the Game script answers "Why you?"

When I found myself standing in front of Grant Goodman and his team, I was ready to tell the story of Gennacode. This meant I was ready to activate the risk, reward, and fairness receptors in a room full of ice-cold financial analysts. But I knew before I had even started that by the time I was finished, these skeptics would have everything they needed in order to say yes to our deal.

It was time to unleash the Pre-Wired Ideas.

THE FEELING OF "I GET IT"

Jenny is the captain of her high school cheerleading squad. She's tall, blond, energetic, and athletic. Always the center of attention, she is dating the star of the football team. She's often cruel to other girls, especially ones who aren't into sports, like the girls involved with band, drama, or computers.

Even though I gave you only around fifty words of description about Jenny, you might feel like you have a decent understanding of her character and how she would act in various situations. This isn't an accident. It's because Jenny fits a stock character archetype you've encountered over and over again in movies, books, and television shows.

You've been exposed to this "cheerleader" stereotype so many times that your brain has actually built an idea receptor for it. When you started reading the description of Jenny, your brain activated this receptor, leading to an immediate feeling of "I get it." This is what happens when your receptors are hit, leading to a pre-wired conclusion, which is exactly what I needed to do now so that Grant Goodman and his tribe would "get it."

PITCHING GENNACODE

"Chronic diseases are the leading cause of death and disability in the United States," I said evenly, leading with the facts. "A hundred and thirty-three million Americans have at least one chronic disease. In recent years, these numbers are going up, not down. Diabetes, Alzheimer's, cancer, arthritis, asthma, stroke . . ."

Everybody looked around the room, uncomfortable with my formidable list of medical deplorables. I had them where I wanted them. Winter was coming, and they felt the stiff breeze on the back of their necks.

"Which one is coming for you?" I asked, looking around the room like the grim reaper seeking out his next soul. "You there." I pointed at a quiet-looking analyst in the middle of the pack. "I bet you have the best insurance possible, right? Your insurance will cover any treatment money can buy, right?" The nervous analyst nodded. "So, what treatment will you buy if Alzheimer's sets in? Because today, there isn't one." The room remained silent; everybody looked at the analyst with the potential incurable disease and looked away, as if they would turn to salt if they kept staring.

"We're living longer than evolution designed us to," I continued. "If you're in this room, mathematically, your life expectancy is eighty-four. But think about it this way: Nature had already planned to wipe you out around age thirty-two. Those extra fifty-two years are an open invitation to chronic disease. And you're not the only one who is outliving your own health limitations. There are 350 million other Americans in exactly the same boat—living too long. Unless we get advanced prediction technologies in place—and start preventing conditions before they occur—the cost of treating these diseases is going to be a third of the entire economy. That's way too much."

I was painting a bleak picture of how bad the future might be if we failed to take action now. That was my Winter Is Coming script. Next, without missing a beat, I jumped right into my 2X script. I looked over at my partner, Professor Rosenberg, and pointed to him, wagging my finger like the grim reaper.

"Professor Rosenberg, how old are you?"

"Seventy-one," he replied.

"And how are you feeling?" I asked him. "I mean, apart from some aches and pains, degrading eyesight, weight gain, hearing problems, heart palpitations, and minor memory loss. . . . Any major diseases creeping up?"

"No, nothing serious," he replied, smiling, but a little hesitantly.

"But how can you *know*? I mean, these good people sitting here," I said, pointing to the analysts, "they are seriously thinking about giving you twenty-two million dollars and then, well, maybe after they do you have a stroke the next day, or you're diagnosed with type two diabetes, or . . . something, anything on that list of fast killer diseases. How can we assure them you've got another five or ten years of good energy and mental health?"

Rosenberg didn't blink; he just stared at the audience, looking as ancient as he seemed to these whiz kids.

"I've got twice the chance of living to ninety as anyone in this room," he said.

"No offense, professor," I said skeptically, "but how are we supposed to believe that? Are you a magician? Do you have a crystal ball? Did you make a deal with the devil?" Next, I pointed at the healthiest-looking kid in the room. About thirty-two years old, muscular, he looked like a real athlete. "What about Chang?" I asked. "Look at him, and now look at yourself. Be *realistic*, professor—how are you going to outlast a guy who takes care of himself like *that*?"

The professor smiled. This was his cue. "Until I see his genetic test, I wouldn't bet on him. The numbers say he could be wiped off the map by the time he's fifty. Since we're talking numbers, I'm already twenty-one years past fifty. Nature programmed me to die long ago, but I'm still here. I've got a PhD in molecular biology and all the equipment a biologist could ever want at my university lab, so I've been treating my genetic weaknesses for decades. And now I've got *this*, which is going to let me easily hit the age of a hundred and twenty." He held up a Gennacode test.

I took the test out of the professor's hand and showed it to the New Icon audience. "Twice as likely to live to ninety as anyone in here," I said thoughtfully, repeating the first word for emphasis: "*Twice* as likely. Thanks to a single test. Going to live to a hundred and twenty unless he gets hit by a bus.

"And since we are contemplating Professor Rosenberg's mortality at present, and now that we are all reassured that he's going to be around for another couple years, let's get to know him a little bit better," I continued. "You can see the highlights of his professional career on his biography, but that doesn't tell the whole story. Sure, it lists all of the academic honors and high-profile speeches he's delivered. But it doesn't show his 1-bedroom apartment in Mid-Wilshire, the 1994 Toyota Corolla he drives, a closet full of cheap black suits from Eastern Europe like this one he's wearing now, and this—I pointed to his wrist—an eighteen-dollar Casio calculator watch. And he flew here on Southwest Airlines in Group C. I know, I sat next to him in seat 37B, worst seat ever—it's by the toilet. Is the professor just cheap? Where's all the money he's earned from all those prestigious awards? There should be at least $5 million somewhere. What happened to it all?

"Let me clear up this minor mystery," I said to the crowd. "You've heard Professor Rosenberg speak here today. You've seen his work. You know the kind of organizations that have awarded him their highest honor. So I'm sure you already know exactly where all his money is—all five point seven million. Of course. It's in Gennacode. So are twelve patents, fifteen years of research, as-sistance from twenty-five PhD colleagues around the world, and most important, the tireless dedication of this man right here." Professor Rosenberg looked up at the people in the room, and I swear he almost blushed. Everyone was smiling at him.

"It's interesting how just a few years ago you would have looked at Gennacode and said, 'Hmm, this is nothing but a ragtag group of international PhD misfits, really just a bunch of "teaching" profes-sors who are playing with genetics, trying to crack the uncrackable code of chronic disease, pretty much the same old story that never goes anywhere,'" I said, rounding third toward home base. "Be-cause when it was just research and math and late-night confer-ence calls about the BRCA genes or the BioSequence technology, we didn't call you for money. The professor wrote those checks month after month, year after year. Real money. Five million bucks. But today, you're looking at the number one company in the field employing high-density microarrays, nanorobotics, and pooled-library multiplexing . . . and a patented enzyme-catalyzed DNA polymerization process.

"And we did all that without you. . . . Now let's cover what we can do *with* you."

I looked around the room and I could tell I'd been successful. The geniuses were silent. Instead of suspicion, they were looking at Rosenberg and me with understanding and appreciation, but we weren't assured of a $20 million check yet. I had to show them what was in it for them. I flipped the projector to show a graph of the company's finances. Thanks to careful spending and a couple of important partnerships with established hospitals, Gennacode already had more than $5 million in revenue.

"Of course," I said, pulling a large stack of folded pages out of my bag, "at the end of the day, what you folks want to know most about is this." I shook the pages in my hand for emphasis, increasing our perceived value and adding to the intrigue with this one gesture alone. "How big can this company get, and how fast? What does the revenue pipeline look like? Will sales be ten million? A hundred million? A billion? I'll tell you right now, it looks pretty darn good. So let's put some hard numbers around this opportunity."

The thick stack of papers quickly made its way around the table. There was a folder for everyone in the room—fifteen dossiers in all. But what nobody realized was that I had a small psychological tactic up my sleeve. These weren't typical hard-to-understand financial projections and reports. Instead, I had printed all the company's contracts, deals, and prospective customer agreements, organized in perfect, tidy rows, exactly as analysts would do for themselves. The revenue projections were atmospherically large, and in each folder I had taped together sixteen sheets of paper like a giant origami map to the secrets of the universe. I had provided information in a way that the analysts were pre-wired to receive it.

As these impossibly large folded printouts were passed around the table and everyone grabbed a copy, the room started to fill with the rustle of paper. And then when the volumes of revenue projections—with supporting evidence of contracts and customer invoices—were unfolded simultaneously, the room got louder, and you could feel the positive energy crackle. I could hear analysts exclaiming, "Oh, this is so cool, check this out!" Paper was flying everywhere as they tried to fully comprehend the extraordinary revenue projections. Everyone loved it—except Grant Goodman, who rose from his chair, glaring at his happy geniuses with dismay.

"Isn't anybody going to ask this guy some *due diligence* questions?" he asked, pointing menacingly around the room. No one said a word. The analysts just shrugged. They had nothing. I had checked every single box. I looked up and saw Grant Goodman staring at me with the most peculiar look on his face. It was like I was David Copperfield and had just made the Statue of Liberty disappear.

An hour later the CFO came out of the deliberation room and looked at the professor and me, stunned. "I don't know what happened in there," he said. "But we just voted to invest in Gennacode, and it's going to be the largest single investment our firm has ever made."

At no point did I tell these investors what to think, or even ask them directly to invest. They decided to do so on their own. This is the awesome power of Pre-Wired Ideas. Even at a circus of money like New Icon, in front of this group of global sophisticates, you can count on everyone—no matter who they are, what their training is, or where they went to school—to respond in exactly the same way when you activate their Pre-Wired Idea receptors.

CHAPTER 5

The Power of Plain Vanilla

My partner Logan is a deal junkie. What kind of deals? Here's a good example. A few years ago we tried to buy the Chicago White Sox because Logan thought we could get the team for a steal. After that, we did buy a $40 million airplane for $30 million, which was a great deal . . . until I realized a single tank of gas was costing me $90,000 and it burned 380 gallons an hour. We bought seventeen hotels, such as the Doubletree in downtown Houston. And then we tried to buy the Tower Records building right out from under the company. Their CEO had a few things to say about that. One of them was no.

Logan goes further, pushes harder, and looks for more creative ways to get a deal done than anyone else out there. We have done twenty-seven deals together, and I always tell him, "This is the last one," but it never is.

The Logan Deals, as I've started calling them, are like action movies starring a venture capitalist with a go-anywhere jet and a no-holds-barred approach to life. He is always looking for his next big win, no matter where it takes him or what the risks. And in a crucial respect, Logan has turned the deal game on its head, because he isn't looking for less risk, he's looking for more—for him, the more millions on the line, the better. If $1 million is good, $10 million is great, and $100 million is golden. He's a man with only two settings: fast and asleep. From the outside, Logan is a well-composed model of success and makes it look easy to be a mogul—but I know firsthand, being a kingpin is far from easy, and closing a deal with him is a bumpy and dangerous ride. What follows is the story of one of the wildest rides I've ever taken.

Over the course of my dealmaking career, I've observed that most people proceed cautiously when chasing a huge financial reward, because they know there is a very real possibility of great loss. This is why most people will pause at critical moments to think about everything that could go wrong (especially when millions of dollars are on the line) and weigh the potential reversal of fortune before they decide whether to go forward.

Not Logan. He immediately goes all-in pretty much without blinking. When Logan is chasing a deal, let's just say he's either in or he's out; there's no maybe.

And this is why I found myself with Logan one Wednesday morning walking through a Chinese marketplace in Honolulu. The Mahalo Marketplace, in the heart of historic downtown Honolulu, is a busy plaza, boasting a colorful combination of shops, an indoor market, and the gastronomic smells of an ethnic food court. We'd arrived on Logan's jet an hour before and he still hadn't told me what the deal was, but I was bracing myself for the moment he revealed his grand plan.

We pushed past a long line of aggressive shoppers at the Tea Hut, walked in front of a small stand with a great selection of exotic spices for purchase, such as "monkey gland five salt ghost pepper mix," and stopped at the Long Life Noodles stall. Logan claimed these would enhance my mental and physical powers.

Was *this* why we had flown here from Beverly Hills?

"Oren, this place is so timeless. . . . It's iconic . . . legendary." (You have to know Logan to understand all this means just one thing: profitable.) He continued, "You can find anything! Look, there—every possible kind of Chinese tea. And right there, dragon's tooth dumplings. And there, shrimp so fresh they are still moving when they serve 'em to you."

Logan had a point. The place was packed with customers. There were lines stretching fifteen deep and more for some of the food vendors. I tried to figure out what he had in mind. It sounded like maybe he wanted to buy a noodle company and franchise it. The two of us had started business ventures in dozens of zip codes over the years, so there was no telling what he might be thinking now. But he was mainly a real estate guy, so noodles seemed a little off base.

"I've never seen anything like this anywhere," Logan continued. "And wait until you see the *rent roll*. There's a yearlong waiting list to get in, five percent annual rent bumps, and the owner keeps two percent of total sales."

I gave a long, low whistle, the kind finance people do when they see a good deal and impressive numbers.

"So what's the deal?" I asked, trying to sound casual as I dug into my soup. Logan's deals always seemed to involve large sums of money and crazy timelines, so I was right to be worried about what was coming next.

Beaming, Logan said, "We can step in to buy the whole thing for forty-two million. We'll acquire it into a special-purpose entity, have our guys update the financials, do a big cleanup, then you sell it for at least fifty million. What do you say, are you in or out?" I almost choked on a Long Life noodle. So that was the deal. We had done a number of these types of real estate deals together already, and making money this way was a simple formula—when it worked:

Step 1: Buy a profitable and stable retail center.
Step 2: Put a few million in to fix it up.
Step 3: Re-calculate the financial projections.
Step 4: Sell it and keep a few million for ourselves.

But we had never put ourselves on the hook for anywhere near $40 million. That was a ton of money. And Mahalo was anything but a slam dunk.

"I don't know, Logan," I said, feeling a bit hesitant. To be blunt, I didn't like the idea of shrimp that still moved when you were eating them, let alone stalls full of fish heads. Plus, I mean, it was Logan. Sure, he's a total bloodhound for deals that have been overlooked by others, ones that are quirky and profitable, but you could always be sure something would come up that wasn't expected.

"Forty-two million," I reminded him, shaking my head. "That's a lot of dough."

There was another reason I wasn't jumping in quite as eagerly as I might have in the past: My wife and our little boy were back in California, living in a nice but small apartment while I was having our family home built in Rancho Santa Fe. The house had started as a simple project, but with the extra two garages, hockey rink, and expanded kitchen the expenses were climbing fast. In fact, just that morning, Vince, the kitchen guy, had been trying to call me about a copper hood for the La Cornue stove he had picked out, but I didn't answer. I knew those stoves were at least twenty-five thousand dollars and I wasn't in the mood to hear about it.

So Logan's proposal was coming at a terrible time for me. I absolutely could not afford to get locked up in a huge deal right now.

"Yeah, but I mean look at this place," he said, waving his hands and looking me dead in the eye. "It's got all the historic bona fides you could ask for. People are going to love it. And it's one of a kind, Oren. The competition can't build another one because, you know, where would you put it? They're not making any more Hawaii."

He had me there. In Texas, you can just build another strip mall two hundred feet down the road from the last one. If you tried that here, you'd end up in the ocean. "All right," I said, since I really didn't want to throw cold water on Logan's enthusiasm. "I'll take a look at the numbers."

Upon further analysis, this deal didn't look bad at all. I was pretty confident I'd be able to sell the place for $50 million, leaving Logan and me to pocket a cool $6 million for the trouble.

"OK," I said after scanning the numbers. "I'm definitely in. But do not sign anything until I can run it by a few investors and make sure there's a market for this monster, so just hold tight." I shot Logan an "I mean it" look so intense that it stopped him mid-noodle. The idea of not moving ahead was not really in his playbook.

"All right," he said, going back to chewing again. "But hurry up; we need to make this happen fast."

TEST-MARKETING THE MARKETPLACE

When entrepreneurs build new apps or websites, they don't have to do much testing before jumping in with both feet and going for it. The total risk involved in building a prototype web application is about fifty thousand dollars. In the business world, this is a small price to pay for launching a product that could be worth millions. This way of doing things is called MVP, or minimum viable product, and it works great when you're writing software in your kitchen with your two best friends and a guy you met at Starbucks. But when you graduate to working a deal worth tens of millions of dollars, "Just do it" is not a great motto. In these situations, when the potential risk is complete financial meltdown, you need to employ a more disciplined process of due diligence.

The reason I was hesitant to jump in with Mahalo Marketplace is the exceptionally high risk. If I wasn't able to find investors who wanted to buy into the deal, then Logan and I would be "locked up," and we'd have to buy it ourselves. In other words, I would own a fifty-two-thousand-square-foot Chinese marketplace, while the bank would come take my house, my cars, and my prized 1975 Roger Staubach game-worn jersey. This was definitely something to be avoided.

To avoid major missteps I have developed a methodical system for conducting due diligence on my deals, as does every company that's about to spend $40 million. Nothing fancy, it's called a Deal Viability Test, and you don't need an MBA or a degree in statistics to figure it out.

Step 1: Speak with about ten potential buyers.
Step 2: Tell them about the best features of the product.
Step 3: Gauge interest.
Step 4: Decide if there's enough demand to keep going.

That's it. I simply pull out my phone, call up a handful of my go-to investors, tell them about whatever deal I'm currently working on, and test their interest. Typically, these are the results:

- Two or three will say, *Yes, I want in!*
- A few others will say, *It's interesting; tell me more.*
- The rest will say, *I told you last time, lose my number!*

If you're lucky enough to get a few yeses on these brief calls, you can move ahead and push the deal through, confident that there is a market for whatever it is you are trying to sell. But I wasn't at all prepared for the response I got about the Mahalo Marketplace.

I sent out an initial query email to some investors to gauge their interest and in less than a half hour I had fifteen calls scheduled—completely unheard of in a business where it's notoriously hard to get decision makers on the phone. And the responses I got to the email were very positive, even enthusiastic.

"Would love to hear more about this. 3:30pm EST?"

"Very interested. Call me between 3 and 4:30."

"Intriguing. Talk now?"

I texted Logan, "Initial response is GREAT," and "Will call you after I talk to everyone." He replied with a smiley face.

For the rest of the afternoon and evening I was on the phone with a total of sixteen investors, and as I made the calls one by one, an interesting pattern started to emerge. In fact, every investor I talked to said exactly the same thing: They loved it *conceptually*, because it was Hawaii, but in reality it had no Starbucks or Jamba Juice and it had some pretty bad Yelp reviews, so in the end: *Nope, not for me. Yeah, it's a cool project, but real quirky; sorry, not interested.* It was definitely cool and exciting, and Hawaii is always worth looking at, but it seemed too much of a risk when they started to learn more about the small vendors, the lack of a Starbucks, and the open-air food stalls. When push came to shove they would rather stick with the tried-and-true.

Whew. I let out an enormous sigh when I hung up with the final investor and crossed his name off the list. I should have been disappointed by the overall response, but in truth I was relieved.

My test-marketing strategy had just saved Logan and me from making a huge mistake.

"I told you, Logan, when it comes to big deals, you have to be cautious. Until I talk to actual buyers, I believe none of what I hear and half of what I see," I said over drinks a short while later. "Turns out there's no way we'd have been able to sell that thing for fifty million. Every investor I talked to said they wouldn't go near it." I pointed a finger at Logan. "This is why we do things my way: careful, scientific, and logical. Measure twice, cut once."

Logan listened intently. He hadn't touched his spicy tuna roll or said a single word for about two minutes. I understood how he felt. Giving up on a deal you've spent time on is one of the most difficult things about this business. Logan had worked with this seller for months and this would be a tough one to get over. I knew he was feeling let down.

"Hey, it's OK," I said reassuringly. "I know you worked hard to line this up. Every deal can't be a winner. We'll find another one."

Logan shook his head. "You're such a hypochondriac," he said in an excited voice, using the term incorrectly. "I already bought the property. I signed the purchase agreement this afternoon."

"You—you . . . *What?*"

Logan had specifically promised not to do this, and promised it over Long Life Noodles!

"Well, that pre-research stuff is always just a formality! You always do it and it's always a green light. Maybe you did it wrong this time." His voice trailed off and we sat there in silence. We both knew what the research meant.

We were now locked up and on the hook for exactly $42 million.

I thought about the house I was having built on the other side of the ocean in California and how it would be repossessed before the dream kitchen was even finished.

SQUIRREL THEORY AND THE SCIENCE OF NOVELTY

Have you ever watched a squirrel explore a piece of litter, a picnic basket, or something left on the ground with food in it? The squirrel has a very specific method to handle this situation. He gets about five feet away, which is as close as he can get to the thing without having a total panic attack. Then he pauses on hind legs for a moment to think and compose himself. Now back on all fours, he advances farther, ever so cautiously getting just . . . a *little . . .* closer, but then *panic!*—he scurries away to hide in a bush. After a brief time-out, he gets the nerve to approach again and gets a little closer this time until, once again—*pitter patter*—he scurries away. This process is repeated many times until finally the squirrel is close enough to stick his head into the bag of chips or whatever it is and discover what is inside. At last, his curiosity is satisfied.

This pattern of behavior is remarkably consistent, whether it's a rabbit, rat, squirrel, or raccoon. And whenever we explore something new, it turns out, it's the same for humans.

After receiving his PhD from Yale in 1951, a young English psychologist named Daniel Berlyne became fascinated with this type of exploratory behavior and dedicated his career to studying it. By subjecting rats to a variety of experiments, he discovered that exploratory behavior changes dramatically depending on the type of object the animal is pursuing. The more radically new and exciting something is, the more likely it is that the animal will decide to explore it . . . but only to a certain extent. Berlyne's research shows that exploratory behavior reaches a peak at a moderate level of novelty and then starts to decline. In other words, mammal brains seem to like things that are a little new and unusual, but not so new and unusual that we don't know how to process it.

Why, exactly, does exploratory behavior always seem to follow this predictable trend of seeking less novelty? The answer involves two conflicting drives: curiosity and anxiety.

You've probably noticed people seem fascinated by things that are new and novel. We have a natural drive toward curiosity. This is no accident. The preference for novelty is wired deep into our brains and can be triggered in an instant. If a squirrel stumbles upon a picnic basket full of sandwiches and potato chips, he has potentially discovered enough food to last him for months if he stores it properly. That is a huge benefit to his survival. But can the squirrel be sure about it? When something is totally new and novel, we don't have much information about it. This means there is a chance the thing could deliver a big reward. So we're programmed to be curious about novel things. The more novel something is, the more curiosity it triggers in us. Curiosity motivates us to approach things and check them out.

This is why people are motivated to hear about your idea (at first) if you introduce it as new and novel and never been done before.

Of course, besides the potential reward, there is also potential risk inherent in novel situations. The picnic basket might not be a basket at all, but a trap that slams shut, capturing the squirrel inside. Novel situations can be dangerous. Because of this danger, we feel anxiety when we encounter novelty. This anxiety makes us more cautious. The more novel the situation is, the more anxiety we feel, and the more cautiously we act.

So how is it that novelty motivates both approach and avoidance at the same time?

Berlyne discovered that the two conflicting drives of curiosity and anxiety are always in operation simultaneously. But at different times and in different situations, one or the other of these drives wins out. Under very novel circumstances (like a strange noise in the middle of the night) anxiety typically prevails and we experience an avoidance tendency. We stay hidden or move away. In more boring or mundane situations (like a mysterious cardboard box) curiosity more often prevails and we experience an approach tendency. We investigate.

You can see these two conflicting drives in action with the squirrel exploring a nearby empty picnic basket. The closer the squirrel gets to the mysterious basket, the more novel the situation becomes for him. At first, when he's far away, anxiety is low and he scurries forward. But as the basket get closer and closer, the novelty level goes up and the squirrel reaches a point where anxiety and curiosity are perfectly balanced. Neither an approach nor an avoidance tendency is experienced. This is where he pauses.

Then he takes one more tiny step forward. And now he has crossed the line and the situation is too novel. The scale tips and anxiety wins out over curiosity. In a rush, the squirrel experiences an avoidance tendency and scurries away to hide in the bushes.

As soon as he reaches the safety of the bushes (a lower level of novelty), the squirrel begins to feel more curiosity than anxiety, so he experiences an approach tendency and scampers toward the basket again, and the process repeats itself.

On each approach the squirrel is able to get a little closer before the urge to retreat overpowers his curiosity. This is because he is gradually getting more and more exposed to the picnic basket, so his novelty sweet spot is slowly shifting closer and closer to the basket. This process might take a while, with many back-and-forth attempts, if the squirrel has never been exposed to a picnic basket before. Eventually, the novelty will wear off to the point where he can stick his head in the basket and see what's inside.

We're not that different from our squirrel friend. Over millions of years these strategies have been imprinted on our DNA. We are preprogrammed to move toward things when we get bored, to increase our novelty level. Similarly, we move away from things when we get too excited, to find a lower level of novelty.

At the end of the day, we're most comfortable with things that are about average.

Ever notice how websites always seem to give you three different price levels? Companies today know that when presented with three ascending options, the vast majority of people will instinctively choose the middle one. So we strategically engineer web pages to present three options: one that is too expensive, one that is too basic or limited, and one that is "just right."

And time and time again customers go with the Plain Vanilla option, the most middle-of-the-road out of the three choices. My problem in Hawaii was that Mahalo Marketplace was 100 percent different from anything investors had seen before. It was in Hawaii and super profitable, which created attraction and the initial urge to approach. But it was also extremely novel, which created anxiety and the avoidance tendency—when they got a little closer, my deal scared them off.

THE ONLY WAY OUT OF A KOBAYASHI MARU

How did I let Logan get me into these kinds of situations? He needed to understand that things were different for me. There was a time when I would have jumped at any deal, no matter how outlandish, if I thought it had a chance of working, but I had my family to think about now. Life had gotten a whole lot more real for me. Logan hadn't even asked about my life. We were always too busy talking about big deals, new airplanes, and empire building.

Logan had signed the contract for this deal and shaken hands with the seller. We were all in. But our research said we were about to be all out. This was the definition of an impossible situation—and exactly how I found myself drinking a beer at the KuaKua, in downtown Honolulu.

Logan had just signed me up for a suicide mission, and the reality of the situation was beginning to sink in. A pint of beer sounded just about right. Unfortunately, this was Logan at the table, so instead of a pint we ordered twelve bottles of Sierra Nevada Torpedo and got down to business. This meant we needed to face some difficult facts about Mahalo Marketplace.

First, my test marketing, which was typically reliable, revealed lukewarm interest from the type of investors we usually worked with. Second, we had already committed to show up in thirty days with $42 million in cash. To admit a mistake now would broadcast to everyone in our industry that we were unreliable and couldn't be trusted to hold up our end of a deal.

"Logan, what we've got here before us is a classic Kobayashi Maru," I said between gulps of Torpedo.

"That test on *Star Trek* that nobody could pass?" he asked, looking morose.

"Yeah, exactly. It's a no-win situation; even Kirk failed the test twice," I said. "Yup, this is a Kobayashi Maru all right."

The Kobayashi Maru was originally designed to test how Starfleet Academy cadets responded to a no-win scenario. It had suddenly occurred to me that Logan and I were living that fictional test, and we had to do something about it, fast. But what?

"So what did Captain Kirk do?" asked Logan.

"He cheated," I said. "He snuck into Starfleet and reprogrammed the computer."

"So let's do that," said Logan, tossing a piece of a rainbow roll into his mouth. "How can we flip the script and reprogram the game?" Over a batch of calamari and seaweed, we struggled to answer that question. What does it mean to reprogram the game when you've got to offload a $40 million marketplace in Hawaii?

Just then, my phone rang. It was the appliance guy for the house I was building two thousand miles away, calling to go over the specs on a bunch of different kitchen appliances, starting with the refrigerator. I sighed, not yet ready to tell him it looked like we were going to have to put the whole project on hold.

"Hey, Vince," I said, trying to cut him off, "I'm kind of in the middle of something right now, can't pick out a fridge."

But Vince ignored me, and kept talking through my attempted interruption. "Here's a quick rundown of what will work for you," he continued with excitement. "We should do the in-fridge fifteen-lens cameras so you can check what's inside remotely from your phone and drag virtual countdown timers over the top of your food to track expiration dates. We'll also do smart grid syncing to schedule defrost cycles. And because you travel quite a bit I'd do a twenty-five temperature zone system with speed chilling. I can get it ordered tomorrow morning and installed by end of week."

"Vince, please. I can't deal with this right now. Just get me the normal regular everyday refrigerator that everyone in my neighborhood gets. Whatever is standard, I'll take it. I really don't need a hologram countdown timer for milk."

There was a chuckle on the other end of the line. "You haven't bought a fridge in quite a while, have you, Oren?" he said, and didn't wait for an answer because the answer was obvious. "Well, these days for a house like yours the standard refrigerators all have speed chillers, smart sync, and reorder apps on the front digital panel. In fact, most of them have laser temperature sensors. So if you want the standard, I guess I'll get you a totally plain-vanilla no-frills Viking. It'll just have the linear compressors and multizone monitors with a backup mini-compressor. That's it, nothing fancy. Plain vanilla. It's $19,980," he said quickly and hung up the phone.

And then a lightbulb went on.

"Virtual smart app countdown timers projected over the top of your food to track expiration dates?" I thought to myself. "Didn't expect that." Now I knew how each of the sixteen investors felt when I had tried to sell them a property that was completely different from the types of properties they were used to purchasing. No wonder they all turned me down.

I had just bought a nineteen-thousand-dollar fridge I hadn't planned to buy. What had this man said to get me to do this? I thought about it for a moment.

"Normal," Vince had said. "Standard . . . plain vanilla." To which I had said: "OK."

Immediately I started replaying the conversation over and over in my mind. What was it, exactly, that had made me buy a fridge with features I hadn't even heard of before? The answer was almost too obvious.

He made the novel (and expensive) features seem normal.

When I slid back into our booth after the phone call, Logan

had a faraway look in his eyes, like he was in a trance. And he still hadn't touched his spicy tuna roll. I grabbed a piece and popped it into my mouth as I tapped him on the shoulder.

"OK," I said, "let's do it."

"What?" Logan asked, perking up.

"The marketplace," I said. "I can sell it. I have an idea."

FROM NOVEL TO THE NEW NORMAL

Imagine you just created a new cold medicine, and you find it's 35 percent more effective than other popular cold meds on the market. Users administer it by vaping rather than taking a pill, so it doesn't have to be swallowed. And it's completely safe to use. Great! You're obviously excited and your mind is going a mile a minute thinking about how popular this new product will be (and how much money you're going to make). Some wealthy friends think it sounds like a slam dunk, so they give you a cash investment and you spend two years working out the details, and when you finally put it on store shelves . . . nobody buys it.

Cold medicine that requires a vaporizer? No thanks. It's just too novel.

For the most part, customers and consumers rely on their tried-and-true suppliers or on their network of friends to suggest new products, rather than trying every new solution that hits the market. Certainly there is a small set of adopters who will try unproven products and take the risk on new ideas and technologies—

but this is not true of the mainstream, middle-of-the-road consumer. **In practice, too much novelty produces avoidance and not the hoped-for attraction effect.**

The grocery store shelves are already lined with a dozen different kinds of cold medication. Your customers have all been seeing the common brands on the shelf for years and years. They already have a medication they use, which their doctor recommended and all their friends use too. These people aren't out looking for a new cold medication that might be one-third better. And they *definitely* don't want to switch from taking pills to vaping, because they've never heard of anyone taking cold medicine like that before; it's too unfamiliar.

To influence people to try a new kind of anything, you first need to find somebody who is willing to listen to you talk about your new thing, whatever it is. At this stage, positioning a project or idea as completely new and original can cause a deceptive amount of interest. These people will listen to the idea. And yes, they'll be intrigued, maybe even engaged and excited. But when it comes to making a decision, they're likely to return to the products and ideas that are already in place and known to work—even if those products and ideas are just average.

This counterintuitive consumer behavior has frustrated thousands of entrepreneurs, who often get fired after telling their board of directors, "It's a great product, so much better than anything else on the market . . . but we are just not selling, and are not going to hit our revenue goals this year."

For more than a decade my colleagues and I have watched

countless companies attempt to sell their products, services, and ideas to all types of buyers. Through interviews, working sessions, and consulting directly with hundreds of executives, I've seen the way most sales presentations go:

1. Salesperson creates excitement by pointing out new features, ideas, or technology
2. Introduces the offering as new and "totally different" from the competition
3. Explains that "this is a new kind of company—we do things differently"
4. Points to industry innovation awards
5. Typically quotes Steve Jobs's commercials or keynote speech: "Here's to the crazy ones . . . The rebels. The troublemakers. The round pegs in the square holes. The ones who see things differently."
6. Moves to the next cliché, comparing their company to disruptive tech giants, Google, Airbnb, Etsy, or Uber ("We're the Uber of toothpaste, really.")
7. Tries to overcome objections and ask for the sale

This rarely works.

So why would sellers consistently choose this particular way to highlight their products? In other words, why are people seemingly preprogrammed to present their ideas as new and different? Because new and different things attract *immediate attention*.

If it sounds new, we can be sure to get a solid look, a return phone call, or an in-person meeting based on novelty. When people hear new ideas, they initially get excited, which provides social validation and gives the seller the illusion of an elevated interest level. But this rise is temporary, and when the exhilaration of new and different wears off, the desire for tried-and-true takes over, and it is surprisingly difficult to get people to actually change their behavior.

One example of this today is with self-driving cars.

For the first time in history, we are seeing the commercial release of the fully autonomous drive-you-anywhere-you-want-to-go car. General Motors makes one, and Ford and Tesla do too. So do Toyota, Nissan, Porsche, and Mercedes, and even Kia will have one soon. Let's assume the cars work like any other, except the one I'm suggesting you buy has no steering wheel you can turn, no brakes you can push, no turn signals or any other controls. The only thing you can touch is the radio knob. So now let me ask— when are you going to buy one?

Your answer to this question will tell me what risks you're willing to take in life. If your reply is, "Did you say no steering wheel or brakes? No way, I'm not buying that until hell freezes over," then you are probably a late adopter, an average consumer who buys around the same time everyone else does. You got an iPhone when the hundredth person in a week pulled one out to show you what they had for breakfast.

Maybe your answer is "I have to have the very first self-driving car available." There aren't a lot of you guys out there, because you people are the crazy ones Jobs was talking about. The crazy ones pursue new technology products aggressively and buy the moment they hear "We have two available—want one?"

But this early versus late adopter market segmentation concept falls apart when the stakes go up. Time and time again my team has found that the bigger and more important a decision is, the more likely it is to be made based on conservative criteria. When lives are at stake, jobs are on the line, and the company has to meet its goals to pay the bills, new and exciting ideas will almost always be considered but passed up. Ask someone who is into driverless cars what they think about fully automated surgeon-less heart surgery. Oh, they'll be interested to hear about it, and they'll approach, but when it's time to commit, the avoidance behavior is going to win out.

This leaves us with a problem. The best method to get people to listen and pay attention to our ideas is to make what we are saying seem new and exciting. But doing so can trigger anxiety and avoidance, and they won't be likely to take action when it counts later on. On the other end of the spectrum, if we make our message seem normal and nonthreatening from the beginning, it's possible nobody will listen to it.

Where's the balance?

The trick is to use a technique called Novelty Chunking to make it seem like your deal is different from "normal" in just one key way, while everything else about the deal is completely Plain Vanilla. Then you show the buyer that what's normal is shifting, and the one key, different thing is really popular today. There is a *new normal*.

Unfortunately, I hadn't yet discovered this foolproof formula when I got stuck staring down the Kobayashi Maru that was Mahalo Marketplace.

A NOVEL IDEA ON MAHALO

Two weeks had passed since Logan signed us up for the suicide mission of selling Mahalo for $50 million. I started sleeping at my desk. I was eating there too. The workload and stress were taking a toll on my health.

Our entire plan for selling Mahalo centered on a single man: Mitch Preston, a prominent real estate investor in Hawaii who basically had a hand in every large real estate deal being done at the time. Mitch was so respected in the market, I knew other investors would follow his lead if I could get him to buy into Mahalo.

But after running my research on this deal and glancing through the specifications of Mitch's most recent investments, I knew exactly what his reaction was going to be: "Yes, it's super profitable, but it's just *too different*." He had a formula that was making him a lot of money. Like all good investors, he would want to stick with what he knew. Mitch's formula was pretty simple: He ran a portfolio of large commercial properties; he held on to buildings for a few years, slowly found creative ways to raise rents, then sold at a profit.

With the clock ticking, we didn't have many choices of serious people at Mitch's level. If he said no, we would have blown our best shot at getting the deal on track.

The fastest way to get Mitch to buy into my deal was to convince him that Mahalo was just like the other properties in his portfolio at the time—that his standard formula would work perfectly on this one. But the more closely I looked at Mahalo, the more problems began to emerge. No way around the facts; this place was nothing like his other properties!

Here was the cold hard reality:

1. We had sixty-eight tenants, almost none of whom had good credit, and they were all on short-term, one-year leases instead of more desirable ten-year leases of the kind you might get from Starbucks.
2. Many tenants were small vendors taking up less than 250 square feet.
3. Tenants did business mostly in cash, which invites IRS auditors to stick their noses in everything.
4. The property wasn't much to look at and lacked what developers call "curb appeal."
5. These vendors sold food that was so fresh, a lot of it was still moving when they handed it to you. Nothing was frozen, packaged, or processed.

So what we had was not ideal, and it didn't fit what investors were normally looking for.

It was time to hit the phones and start some additional research. I was making call after call, searching desperately for a way to highlight Mahalo as the new normal.

"Hey, Chad," I would say when I got a real estate analyst on the phone. "Just wanted to see what the latest trends are that you're seeing in large commercial real estate deals. What have you come across lately?"

"Beverly, quick question," I said to a leading real estate broker. "If you had to guess, what would you say the next ten big deals will look like in the market?"

"Brett, my main man, what's new in your market right now?"

I jotted any interesting responses down on Post-it notes and whiteboards. The key would be to find a trend that I could use to put this new deal in context. Meanwhile, Logan hired a couple of analysts named Jon and Mike, and I had them reading through mountains of paperwork on other big real estate deals currently on the market around the world.

We kept asking the same two questions: What parts of our deal would attract Mitch and what parts would push him away? In other words, "How is this deal the same as Mitch's other deals?" and "How is this deal very different and unique?" The plan was to find the perfect way to explain Mahalo as the new normal.

But as the days ticked by and the meeting drew closer Jon and Mike grew increasingly agitated. "This is a waste of time!" Mike exploded at me with about twenty hours left until the meeting. "We need to be writing the offering memorandum, not looking for a needle in a haystack with all this psychological BS."

"Yeah," Jon chimed in. "This is a joke. We've spent the last week reading about all-glass malls and malls with luxury apartments in them and Disney malls and that insane mall in Dubai with a ski slope in it. We should have been focusing on the mall we're actually trying to sell."

"OK," I said, nodding. "You guys are right. Why don't you both get a few hours of sleep while I look over all of this once more? Then we'll throw the proposal together in the morning." They agreed and left the room in a huff.

I sighed. As much as I hated to admit it, Jon and Mike had a point. We had wasted a ton of time researching other deals and now had no time left to create our pitch deck. To make matters worse, we hadn't uncovered any brilliant insights during the research that we could use to get Mitch on board. None of the lucrative malls of the past few years looked anything like Mahalo.

My knees ached and I had to slide into a nearby chair. My breaths came quick and shallow. For the first time ever I had genuinely gotten myself in too deep. Or Logan had. I wasn't even sure whose fault it was anymore. And now I was just hours away from completely embarrassing myself, sinking our firm while broadcasting to the banking community that we couldn't close deals or meet commitments on time.

Jon's and Mike's words echoed in my head.

"Waste of time."

"Needle in a haystack."

"This is a joke."

And for some reason, I kept thinking about the last thing Jon had said: ". . . all-glass malls and malls with luxury apartments in them and . . . a ski slope."

Wait a minute. A number of the large deals on the market at the time were malls with some type of big differentiator. These weren't your regular malls; they all had something to set them apart. Malls with a *theme*. I looked up that mall in Dubai, and implausibly it did have its very own ski slope. It's called Mall of the Emirates, and it has a hundred restaurants and eighty luxury stores, and is home to Ski Dubai, the Middle East's first indoor snow park. It had recently been named the World's Leading Shopping Mall at the World Travel Awards. And it was profitable too. Investors had put $218 million into it and were taking a lot more out.

I shot to my feet and started rifling through a stack of papers on my desk, pulling files that fit with this potential theme. There was a mall under construction in Thousand Oaks, California, that the developers were calling a village—which just meant that they had built some residences in addition to the shops. There was the mall Jon had mentioned, Westfield Century City, which had the same shops as a normal mall but had an outdoor bazaar look and feel. There was a mall that just sold in Canada where the theme was pirates, and there was even a large pool in the center with a giant pirate ship in it.

All big deals, all malls with a theme.

This was exactly what would make Mahalo work. I could easily show Mitch that this property was *themed* as an authentic Chinese open-air market. I could chunk the many novel features surrounding Mahalo as belonging within this same category. Then I could suggest that this was the new normal for shopping centers. Many of the big malls on the market today are themed as well.

If you've ever had the experience of seeing the answer you seek crystallize in front of you just in the nick of time, you know how I felt at this moment—*ecstatic*. I turned the song "Eye of the Tiger" on full blast and discoed around the office for about three minutes. Then I buckled down. I now had a few hours to actually write the pitch and get it ready to deliver to Mitch.

CHUNK THE NOVELTY INTO ONE CATEGORY

Every buyer has a slightly different level of tolerance for risk, or what I call a *novelty preference point*. Once you push a buyer past this preference point, anxiety, stress, and a host of problems start to occur and he or she will begin to back off.

My team and I have found that the best way to introduce new features, sexy concepts, wild ideas, and forward thinking without going past the novelty preference point (so that it will appeal to virtually any buyer) is to use Novelty Chunking. As I've mentioned, this is the practice of grouping everything new and potentially scary about your deal into a single category and then telling the buyer that your deal is just like every other deal in your industry, except for one key aspect that's totally new.

The idea is to carefully control how new and risky your deal seems to the buyer, because buyers add up risks, almost like a point system. If you have many new and unproven features and ideas, then you have many risks. It's as if it doesn't matter how big the risk is; it matters *how many* risks there are. To control the way risk is perceived, create a list of all the novel or scary things about your idea. Then figure out some way all these items are related to each other. This becomes the "chunk" that you'll use to explain how your idea is different in one key way from the status quo.

For instance, Microsoft Word is by far the most widely used word processing program today. In fact, one of the top ten phrases used in business is "I sent you the Word doc." It's hard to get more Plain Vanilla than that. But let's say you were trying to get someone to switch from Word to a newer word processor, like Google Docs.

There are plenty of things about Google Docs that are different from Word. It is accessed through a web browser; you don't *download it* or *start it up*. Documents are saved to your Google account, not your hard drive. In Google Docs, multiple people can be working on the same document at the same time, a feature Word does not support very easily. But Google Docs didn't become popular because Google promoted these and seventeen other new things about it. Instead they built buzz on just one: Everyone works in one document; see changes immediately.

So to write a Plain Vanilla script for Google Docs you would first focus on how similar it is to Microsoft Word. "Hey, look, Microsoft Word is fantastic. It's the perfect desktop word processor, and I would never change a thing about it. The simple interface with the ruler and toolbar at the top of the screen makes word processing a breeze. Google Docs keeps everything that makes Word great. The text editor feels almost identical. You can save, edit, spell-check, word-count, comment, and even track changes."

Once you've established the many aspects of the product that haven't changed, it's a simple matter to introduce the Novelty Chunk: "But there is one key difference that sets Google Docs apart from Word. It is cloud based. This means the document lives in the cloud and multiple people can access it through a web browser from anywhere on the planet simultaneously."

In essence, you combine everything new about your idea into one Novelty Chunk. Then you explain to your buyer that the status quo is great and works just fine. Acknowledge that they probably aren't looking for a replacement. Finally, introduce the one way your idea is novel and show why this novelty is good—and how it's the same thing nearly everyone is doing (collaborating on projects in the cloud is the new normal).

And that was exactly my plan for selling Mahalo Marketplace. Except I only had a few hours to pull it all together.

THE MAHALO MARKETPLACE PITCH

By the time Jon and Mike showed back up at six a.m., I'd already figured out most of the details. "It isn't enough to just build a regular mall anymore," I said when they walked in. "You need a big extra feature, a theme." I spread six files on the table. Jon and Mike looked on, eyes bleary. "Here's our examples. We frame this as the trend right now. Then we show that Mahalo is no different from any other new mall. By the numbers it is a standard mall. The theme is that it is an open-air market with fresh seafood and authentic Chinese small goods." They weren't happy about the early call time, but they got to work right away. We buckled down for four hours and pumped out a pitch deck.

Then Logan and I, extremely sleep-deprived, showed up at Mitch's office to meet with the one man who could save us from our Kobayashi Maru. There hadn't been any time to write a complicated pitch, so what we ended up telling him was very simple.

"You've probably noticed the latest trend in large commercial real estate," I started. "Shopping malls with a theme. There's this ski resort mall in Dubai, this pirate ship mall in Canada, this all-glass mall in L.A." I casually tossed the files for these projects onto Mitch's desk as I referenced each one. "These projects all sold in the last year for over a hundred million each."

"And we've got the next one," said Logan enthusiastically. "It's right here in Hawaii. By the numbers, it's a standard, Plain Vanilla shopping mall like you might find anywhere. It's insured, bonded, up to spec on health code, and seismically sound. It checks all the liability boxes from an investor standpoint."

"*But* there's something very unique about this property," I continued. "It doesn't *feel* like a regular old mall when you step inside. It feels exactly like an authentic Chinese open-air market. The vendors are all small and quirky, selling exotic and fresh items from all over the world. The layout is based on an actual market in China that dates back to two hundred BC. But the location is smack in downtown Honolulu and all the permits are good for at least another twenty years, just like the other properties in your portfolio."

"Yep," Logan repeated. "Plain Vanilla. No frills. Straight up the middle."

"We're selling it in the next five days," I said with as much confidence as I could muster.

And we stopped talking.

Mitch leaned back in his chair and stroked his chin. He was over seventy years old, and now that I was up close, he almost looked frail. But he clearly had an incredible mind for real estate. "Financial projections?" he asked.

"Page thirty-four," I said.

He flipped through the pitch deck and examined the page where we'd laid out the revenue pipeline, rent roll, annual bumps of 5 percent, and low monthly expenses, and we were even up front about the HVAC needing an update within five years. The guy didn't even get out a calculator. He just started crunching numbers in his head and muttering to himself.

I looked at Logan, who shrugged at me.

Finally, after what seemed like ten minutes during which none of us uttered a single word, Mitch broke his state of trance and looked back up at us.

"I like it," he said.

My natural instinct was to say, "*Great!* We can take you down and show you the property immediately." In other words, to suggest a next step and try to lock him into a yes. That's how sales works, right? You always have to be in control and push the buyer to do things on your agenda, right?

Except I resisted that urge. All I said was: "How do you see us working together on this?"

Later that afternoon Mitch wired us $10 million. He never

even walked the property; our third-party independent reports were good enough. With Mitch on board and his money in escrow, we hit our Rolodex hard and easily had the remaining investors lined up within a week.

A happy ending for everyone, kind of. I had a wife and kid back at home who hadn't seen me in two weeks. On the plus side, they would still have a house to live in, thanks to my share of the $6 million from the deal.

As Logan's jet took off and we headed back toward California, I couldn't help but breathe a huge sigh of relief. That was way too close a call.

I pulled out my phone to check a few of the temperature zones in our new refrigerator and make sure the beer was going to be ice cold when I got home. Yep, 34 degrees, just the way I like it. "This isn't so fancy," I thought to myself. Just a regular fridge like everyone uses in my neighborhood . . . Plain Vanilla.

CHAPTER 6

Leveraging Pessimism

I t was 2:41 a.m. The caller ID read ZERO GRAVITY. My phone was supposed to be in airplane mode because we were on vacation, but I'd left it on because of the fires burning in California near our home, and now, at a time of night that I generally find to be the most tranquil, it was vibrating and ringing like an air-raid siren.

It was February. A heavy snow was falling. We were in Vail, Colorado, with our four-year-old son, enjoying a family ski trip. "No calls, for sure," I had promised. *Just me, you, and the baby.*

But at two a.m. I had to pick up *this* call because I had three million bucks riding on Zero Gravity.

"Oren, I need you to help. I am ready take company public but need sniper right now. You help me get best one OK?"

"Wait a sec," I whispered, trying not to disturb the beautiful woman sleeping next to me (as if the phone erupting into a chorus of "Barracuda" a few moments earlier had not already done so). I threw on shorts and quietly headed down the hallway toward the living room in our suite, with a view of the slopes. I had a feeling I wasn't going to be carving fresh powder in the morning as planned.

Now I was ready to ask some questions of my own. "Anton, is your hundred thousand dollar watch broken again?"

"Ha ha. No time for you funny guy, Oren."

This was Zero Gravity's real name, Anton Kolisnychenko. A few years ago I had met Anton in a bar in his native Ukraine when I had lost my guide earlier in the day and was stumbling around downtown Kiev without a translator, a charged cell phone, or a clue. As day turned to night, I was getting very, very thirsty, so I slipped into a modern-looking bar. They served vodka and just one type of beer—Genesee Cream Ale (worst beer on the planet).

Anton was the only other soul in the bar who spoke any form of English. He helped me translate the menu and he ordered potatoes and some weird dish called golubtsi, which I quickly discovered does *not* mean "delicious hamburger." We shared a meal of golubtsi, selyodka, and kishke. And formed a friendship.

But now that friendship was being tested.

"You told me call if I need you. Well, now need you. You meet me tomorrow," said Anton.

This wasn't a question. And as usual with Anton, there were no pleasantries, no apologies for calling at two a.m. Just typical straight-to-the-point Anton, with whom an early-morning call always ended with "You need to meet me in a Soviet Bloc country twelve thousand miles away for such-and-such random emergency situation."

But sometimes there was three million dollars at the end of that twelve-thousand-mile trip. And sometimes there was just a hard-to-pronounce cabbage roll. In the future, I had to get better at figuring out which was which.

"I am lost my prize sniper right before yesterday. Without superstar number one sniper, I can't win XXL tournament."

That hit the fear center of the brain, and for good reason. XXL was a gaming tournament in which $3 million in prize money could be won by the best teams, and until a moment ago, Anton had one of the best teams. In fact, I had recently made a large business bet that he would win this very tournament.

"If I don't win, can't fund my software company, can't take company public like we plan." While Anton rambled, I flipped on the light, temporarily blinding myself, and began fumbling with the hotel's in-room coffee maker.

"Oren, you tell me, please," he said more desperately than I'd ever heard him sound. "What am I do now? This is what you say, *situation crazy*."

I slid a cup under the coffee maker. In just a few minutes I had gone from fast asleep to hearing the words "Hey man, you need to find me a world-class sniper or we're going to lose a shot at three million bucks."

And there was even more riding on it than $3 million. You see, we needed that money to buy another company, and take the combined companies public on the Nasdaq stock exchange—another way of saying we needed $3 million to get $20 million and hopefully make $100 million. The exact details of how this works aren't important; what matters is that we had a plan, and we needed the XXL tournament winnings to get the whole process started. It was XXL or die.

"Wait a second, you already have a sniper," I said, starting to wake up as caffeine made its way into my central nervous system. "What happened to the fat Asian kid in the Van Halen shirt? He's awesome."

"Oh, you mean GummiBear? Yes of course, he's best in world. But Oren, *I quit that team.*"

"Wait. *What?*" Anton leaving his team was like Tom Brady in his prime quitting the Patriots. This was indeed situation crazy. "Why would you leave your team, Anton?"

He gave me a long, rambling rant about unfair treatment at the hands of the company that managed his team, while I placed him on mute and cursed him loudly. Finally, he reached the end of his monologue and I took the phone off mute to get down to business.

"OK, let me see if I've got this straight," I said, rubbing my forehead and trying to piece together the various strands of Anton's story. "You got sick of management putting you on a constant game rotation with no rest, so you organized a mutiny but it backfired, and your contract got terminated, so you pulled together a new team . . . but you don't have a sniper. Without a good sniper the whole deal is up in smoke. And now, at two-thirty a.m. on a

Tuesday while I am in Colorado on a family vacation, you want me to find you a sniper?"

"I know you can do it, Oren Klaff. You are the only person I can call. I am so much believing in you. And it will only take you few hours. Then you go back to happy snow vacation. I can't win without best sniper. If I don't win XXL money, it all goes up in gas."

"Smoke," I corrected him.

"I quit smoke last year," Anton said.

"Never mind. So who's the best sniper in the world?" I asked.

"Mac Jones 'Bulletz for Breakfast,'" he replied. I waited for him to laugh or somehow indicate that he was joking, but he didn't.

"So he's the guy we need?"

"Absolutely. It's Bulletz or we definitely lose."

I wasn't quite understanding. "Why don't you just ask him to play with you? I mean, you're an eSports celebrity. And you make millions for your teammates. Everybody in the world wants to play on your team. Why would he say no?"

"I already ask him," said Anton. "He says already on good team. He is celebrity with very good contract and not want to change middle of season. Maybe next year, maybe not."

It was now Tuesday morning at 3:15 a.m. I was not too happy. "Just tell me how to find him. That's all I need to know," I said flatly, hiding my frustration.

"He'll be at Gamecon tomorrow in Las Vegas," said Anton, excited to have me once again solving his problems. "This is why I say, please come; it's only short flight. I'll send the 604-LX."

That meant a Bombardier Challenger 604 aircraft was headed

my way. At 48,000 pounds, 20 seats, a small bedroom, with shower, and 600 mph cruising speed, that's as good as it gets.

"OK, comrade," I said. "I'll meet you there for a few hours, and then it's back to the slopes for me, got it?"

"No, but thank you," said Anton, a.k.a. Zero Gravity, misunderstanding me on purpose (his way of doing things). "See you in few hours because plane there soon. It is just easy; meet pilot at Beaver Creek. OK very good." *Click.*

I sighed. Anton, if nothing else, was definitely an optimist.

THE PESSIMISM PROBLEM

Everyone loves an optimist. A positive outlook is one of the most important traits we look for in friends, employees, leaders, and especially salespeople. We teach our kids that a can-do attitude is the key to success. And almost every self-help book starts with the mantra "You can do it!" (once you meditate, visualize what you want, and eliminate all forms of negativity). After all, positive thinking works wonders, right? *We actualize what we visualize.* Maybe and maybe not.

It's certainly enjoyable to talk about what will happen once the deal is closed, the money is in the bank, and the business plan starts happening. It's fun to imagine a future where our problems are long gone, we live in a dream house, everyone adores us, and we are showered with praise. Psychologists simply call this the

Optimism Mind-set: the belief that generally speaking, good things are going to happen soon, very soon.

A positive outlook can motivate people toward incredible accomplishments. Optimists are the ones who put a man on the moon last century, and in this century, they'll put another one on Mars. Optimists climbed Mount Everest, created nuclear energy, and sequenced the human genome. Optimists are good at motivating and attracting others to join their cause.

So if you had to guess, what types of professionals are the most optimistic?

There's no question about it: entrepreneurs and salespeople. By definition, their job is to seed optimism. They're programmed to promote a vision of the future in which your biggest problems are solved, your life becomes easier, and your dreams are checked off one after the next. Just buy now and you will look better, feel better, make more money, get the girl, be parent of the year, and rise in the social hierarchy to become a beloved role model for the regular citizens to admire.

Given the nature of their profession, salespeople are programmed to be optimistic and push you in that direction too. But does projecting optimism work as well as we think?

Just consider how the typical sales sequence goes:

1. Introduce the product; explain the offer.
2. Be exceedingly optimistic; encourage the buyer to feel good about the product.

3. Try to close: "So what do you think? Do we have a deal today?" At which point the buyer raises his or her concerns and objections.

4. Work hard to crush each objection, one by one. Tell the buyer none of his fears will materialize, and all of her dreams will come true.

5. Try to close again—and keep trying (try till you die).

The problem with this pattern is it is closer to debate and argumentation than it is to selling and convincing. The result? Even if the buyer relents and says yes, he hasn't really bought in; most likely he didn't have the time or energy to debate the purchase any further with you, so he said yes to end the standoff and get out of the conversation. But he may or may not have had any real intention of going through with it. This is why it's such a common occurrence for salespeople to think they've closed a deal, only to watch it fall apart as time goes on.

Pure optimism—the kind that bubbles up from the emotional core of salespeople—actually creates stress for the typical buyer. Bursting enthusiasm and excessive positivity can disrupt the buyer's decision-making process and violate his or her sense of autonomy—something you never want to do.

Let me flip the script for you: **It's pessimism, not optimism, that is the formula for success in sales.**

Pessimism gets a bad rap as the evil opposite of optimism. It's not. What pessimism actually does is provide an alternative point of view, and it's one the buyer has to consider before making a purchase decision that sticks and doesn't result in buyer's remorse.

When it comes to making a deal in which there's a lot on the line, buyers always go through a period of skepticism and unease before they ultimately decide they feel good enough to move forward. They must consider how the partnership with you might fail; how things might not work out the way you say; and how, by choosing you over someone else, they may actually lose some (or all) of their money. You should not fight this process, but instead guide them through it.

I realize this might seem counterintuitive and self-destructive. After all, it doesn't exactly sound like the positive thinking they teach at a "Win Friends and Influence People" seminar. To influence people, we're supposed to minimize all negative thoughts, leaving buyers excited and enthusiastic about investing in us and our ideas, right? Not exactly. The possibility of failure enhances a buyer's motivation to act.

There is a kind of self-satisfaction to pessimism. Thinking about obstacles and the many things that might go wrong in a deal is healthy and reassuring, because nothing in life is perfect, and buyers are searching for that imperfection to decide if they can live with it or not. If you hide the negatives, the sale cannot proceed. Until the negatives are out in the open, the buyer's spoken or unspoken state of mind is "What's the catch?" Therefore, pessimism is not a type of negative thinking that needs to be argued with, overcome, and destroyed. Instead, it should be invited and cultivated.

Think about it this way. When you pressure a buyer to express optimism and move ahead with your deal before they feel ready, it threatens their feeling of autonomy. People react negatively when their autonomy is restricted in any way, because, as I established early in this book, we are hardwired to want to feel we are making our own decisions through a period of personal reflection, on our own time, and without pressure by others. You must give the person you are doing business with a feeling of autonomy so they feel totally free to object, demur, and disagree, knowing that you aren't going to be jumping on their case to overcome objections.

Giving a buyer autonomy doesn't mean giving up control, but most people feel they have to choose one or the other. Have you ever seen a good presentation that is well organized, insightful, and persuasive but at the last moment fizzles like a damp match that won't light, failing to close the deal? The last few seconds probably involved one of these statements:

- "So . . . what do you think? Is this something you would be interested in?"
- "That's my pitch, so let me turn it over to you, are there any questions?"
- "Does all this make sense? What are your thoughts and feelings about moving ahead with the purchase?"

These are common ways to end a presentation—I've seen it a thousand times over. The problem with these kinds of statements is that they do nothing but put absolute control in the hands of the buyer. Next, the astute buyer will supply a laundry list of reasons why he can't go any further today, and say exactly what every buyer is preprogrammed to say: "This looks good. We don't have any more questions right now, but if you give us all the information by email, we'll discuss it internally and get back to you in the next few weeks."

A few weeks? And who exactly is "we"?

Clearly, you cannot give the buyer complete control to decide how to proceed with you and your deal, because it may well be the last you hear from them. The goal is not to have weeks of follow-up calls and frustrating interactions. The goal is to create Inception today . . . *Now.*

I've found that the solution is pretty simple: Give a buyer permission to start questioning you and your deal, **but first teach them exactly what to question about it**.

Pessimism + Autonomy + Expertise = Inception

You have to be careful, however, because telling anyone what to question and what not to question can be viewed as if you're telling them what to think. And when a buyer sees an obvious manipulation, he or she starts to back away.

Evidence of this comes from the auto industry, which historically used high-pressure tactics and trained their salespeople to never take no for an answer. Today, it's quite different. Every major auto manufacturer has gone to standardized pricing published online, and low-pressure deal making. They have learned that pressure backfires.

Buyers want control (or at least the illusion of it) over the buying process. When a buyer feels controlled by you, he takes a step back, or leaves the negotiation entirely. Any feeling of psychological control, time pressure, scarcity pressure, social pressure, or other typical sales tools causes buyers to simply back away.

But you wouldn't need to control anyone if you had a way to put in place a sort of hidden boundary, so the conversation stayed focused on what's important and stayed away from distraction. Imagine an invisible fence, like the ones used to keep a dog in the yard, which would contain a buyer's questions about what really matters. Inside the invisible fence are all the facts that need to be accepted, topics open for discussion, issues you are happy to discuss. Outside the fence are off-limits topics, things that don't matter, and time wasters. And if you set this invisible fence properly, the buyer won't realize you've erected the boundaries and will accept them as a natural part of the conversation.

In Las Vegas for the big tournament, I was about to use this approach to help Anton recruit a world-class sniper for his *Counter-Strike* team. But there were a few twists in store I didn't see coming.

PICKING OFF A STAR SNIPER

"There he is," said Anton, taking my arm and pointing in the direction of a kid who fit the perfect gamer stereotype: dyed blond hair with a few purple streaks, three-hundred-dollar sneakers, black hoodie, drinking a Mountain Dew. A group of fans surrounded this eSports "athlete," pushing for autographs as they might a football or baseball star. It seemed a bit much, because, after all, these were just video game players.

To be fair, if any video game player deserved this star treatment at any tournament ever, it was this one. Mac "Bulletz4Breakfast" Jones was one of the best snipers in the world. He was a master of efficiency and knew where to be in the game at every instant and what to do from any spot on the map. If you needed to destroy enemy positions, win games, and rack up tournament points, you needed Bulletz or someone like him.

All this is to say: There wasn't a team that *didn't* want Bulletz. If we were going to have any hope of convincing him to come play for us, we'd have to offer him something other teams simply couldn't—or weren't thinking about. But what could that possibly be?

Anton and I spent a few energy-drink-fueled hours cooking up the best pitch we could come up with. The plan was to focus on how we could provide for him in the long term, whereas his current team was thinking only about the short term. We thought it was compelling and had a chance to sway him. Now we were going to find out as we elbowed through the semicircle of fans and presented ourselves.

"What do you guys want?" Bulletz asked as soon as we got within eyesight. "You're poison right now, Anton. Don't even stand near me. I could get fired just for talking to you." Bulletz looked nervously around the lobby to see who might be watching or recording this conversation. "I already have a team," he added with a tone of finality, and started to move away from us.

"Thought you might be able to use a couple of friends like us, given your current situation and what people are saying—because it's not all good stuff," I said, shrugging casually. It was crucial that we didn't look needy. Whiz kids like Bulletz could smell desperation a mile away.

"Maybe you not so secure as you think if you no even allowed to talk to us," said Anton. "We came because have something you want, you need, something you can use . . . if you're going to keep playing the game."

We had just said to Bulletz, in effect, "Industry people are talking about you and there's a problem brewing. We can help get ahead of it—and even solve it."

The idea was to cause an inkling of impending doom to creep into Bulletz's thinking. With these two statements, we had used the twin psychological hooks that will always get the attention of a star competitor, whether an athlete, surgeon, entrepreneur, or executive. While almost nothing works on everyone, you'll be surprised how effective this can be to get someone's attention: arousing their curiosity by threatening their social ranking and then offering a valuable secret. When these elements are combined, no one can resist at least taking a look. It's as close to a universal *curiosity formula* as you can get.

When you imply that someone's position in the dominance

hierarchy and social order is changing, they snap to attention. It's the first rule of stardom that every celebrity desperately needs to know what is being said about him or her by others, and is highly tuned to gossip coming from fans and peers. Second, every star knows intuitively that you're only as good as your last win, so they are on the constant lookout for valuable information provided by a competitor. Quarterbacks want to know what other quarterbacks are doing to prevent injury in running plays. CEOs of Fortune 500 companies want to know what other CEOs are doing to keep stock prices stable while interest rates are rising. And gamers want to know how other gamers are making money in the emerging eSports industry.

We had taken the first step in the recruitment of Bulletz, but we couldn't push him to switch teams at that moment; he was barely willing to talk to us. This was going to be a slow boil. In the end, it would have to be his decision, or at least feel like it was. We needed Inception.

"What are you talking about?" he said. "I don't need anything. I'm at the top of my game. Look around—I've got the best contract of any player at this tournament." His pride was a little too defensive. He wasn't used to thinking about his future pessimistically, and doing so had rattled him enough to get him to pay attention to us and start talking.

We had moved away from the crowd as security guards pushed the fans off and they scattered, looking for easier autographs.

"That contract of yours isn't going to last another year," said

Anton, because he couldn't help adding an extra jab. "You're twenty-five years old, that's the expiration date for a gamer."

He was right. As living proof, Anton was already thirty-five and hadn't been a competitive player for years.

"Your numbers are down," I said, leaning in conspiratorially, like a good cop giving him advice for his own good. "Nobody's winning streak lasts as long as they think it will.

"Let us show you what we have and you can decide for yourself if it's valuable," I continued. "We are building a gaming team that makes money year after year, and we don't worry about winning or losing this tournament or that one. Look at Zero," I said, pointing to Anton. "He's a mediocre player compared to these kids, right? What would you pay him, seventy-five thousand? Or less?"

Bulletz nodded and winced at the same time, as if this was a very low salary to do the "hard work" of playing video games—but it was also the right number.

"Well, this year he's going to make three million. We could help set you up like this—a better long-term picture for yourself, something that will work when you're as old as Zero here. We have a different way of looking at things for players like you, a way that builds a lot of wealth, win or lose."

"OK, I'll listen, but it has to be *fast*," Bulletz said, suddenly looking a little nervous. I almost felt bad for him. When you took away all those digital guns and grenades, he was just an uncertain kid who was always one big loss away from moving back to his hometown in the Midwest to work at an Apple store. "You want me to leave my management and take a shot with you? That's professional suicide. If your team fails, no one will touch me."

"No, you're wro—" Anton started, and stopped when he felt me stepping on his foot to keep him from talking. If he started countering every one of Bulletz's objections, he would just turn it into a battle of two big egos, and in that scenario Bulletz would never agree to join Anton's team. The only way to get this kid to come on board was to let him feel all the negative thoughts he was experiencing and process them, and help him realize our deal was better for him. It had to be his own decision, without Anton bullying him into anything at all. I had to cut this short until I could talk to Anton about the importance of pessimism.

"Listen, kid, you've had a great five-year run," I said. "You're a legend. You know the game better than anyone. I mean, you're right, you don't need us right now. But you still need to see what we have."

"OK," he said quietly, "I'll meet you during the preliminary round one."

DROP THE DOME TO CONTAIN THE PESSIMISM

Autonomy and pessimism is a dangerous combination. The problem is that once your buyer starts thinking about negative aspects of you and your deal, he might start to question things you don't want him questioning, for which there are no good answers and which don't matter anyway. After you grant the buyer full autonomy to think, do, and say anything that comes to mind, you can no longer control him. The solution is to set up invisible boundaries ahead of time and get your buyer to accept them. Then, when you do grant him autonomy, he will naturally confine himself within the "do not cross" lines you created, without even realizing he is doing it.

Watching a classic Jim Carrey movie can teach us something about how this works. In the film *The Truman Show*, the main character, Truman Burbank, played by Carrey, comes to realize he has been living his entire life beneath a giant dome constructed by television producers. Everyone Truman has ever known turns out to be an actor, and he has unwittingly been the star of a TV show his entire life. It takes him decades to realize he has been living under a dome, discovering it finally when his sailboat crashes into plywood painted to look like the distant horizon.

This, of course, is a dramatic Hollywood example, but it illustrates a fundamental truth: Humans are generally slow to question boundaries if we don't notice them being set.

If you have ever flown on a commercial airliner, you have heard the safety instructions at the beginning of the flight. One instruction concerns the oxygen masks, which will drop down from the overhead compartment in the event of a sudden depressurization at altitude. In that talk, you are warned to put on your own mask before trying to assist someone else. Do you know why? It doesn't matter *why*, because they aren't asking you to debate this topic. They're telling you how it works and if you don't like it, feel free to get off the plane. (Of course, the answer is that at high altitude there is very little oxygen in the air, and the brain can survive for only a few seconds without supplemental oxygen, so in the time it takes to help someone else who is confused and struggling, you could both pass out and die and will be of no help to others.)

When boundaries are already in place ahead of time, or explained as the industry norm, we don't question them. But when someone tries to push a seemingly arbitrary limit upon us out of the blue, we resist. If you want to change the rules, no problem—you simply have to do it very slowly, little by little, so your buyer doesn't notice. Experimental psychologists describe this with names like "change blindness," "choice detection," or "the flicker paradigm." No matter what you call it, study after study has shown that if the rules are imposed on us slowly enough, we don't even notice. If control is taken away in a certain pattern and at a slow-enough pace, it is invisible to us.

So when it's time to let buyers talk about the ideas you've presented and consider the implications for themselves, it's important that they feel unhindered and able to steer the conversation in any direction they want. At the same time, you need to set invisible boundaries that contain their questions within a certain area. But you have to do this gradually so that the buyer doesn't feel constrained by you.

My team and I have discovered how to impose boundaries on your buyer before you turn the conversation over to them to talk about whatever they want. If you do this in just the right way, they won't notice any limitation at all. Then, when you grant them autonomy, they'll stick to the areas you've already outlined and will not deviate.

Why would a buyer accept conversational boundaries that are imposed by you? Well, of course, you aren't going to make it quite so obvious. You aren't going to just come right out and tell the buyer that you'd like them to avoid certain topics. If you did that, they wouldn't be able to think of anything *but* the off-limits areas; you will have created a Do Not Touch button that everyone will immediately reach for.

Instead, we need a more subtle way to impose boundaries.

THE BUYER'S FORMULA

In my deals, I use a seven-step Buyer's Formula to lay down "do not cross" lines. It's important to understand that not every fact, item, subject, and issue a buyer wants to talk about is worth discussing. For example, let's say he found another person who offers a much lower price than you. Well, that's great; he should go buy from them. I say this because nearly every professional salesperson I know refuses to have a price held over their head in a negotiation. Most of the time price is the least important part of the deal, because it's the *terms* of the deal that really matter like financing, delivery timeline, and length of contract. And have you ever heard a potential buyer say, "Of course, I can't make a decision now because I'll have to convince my partner first"? OK, but why should I present my offer, negotiate the terms, and bargain in good faith knowing there's a shadowy partner out there whom I haven't met, am not going to talk to, and don't know anything about, or who may not even exist? In the final analysis, every buyer wants to discuss and debate a wide range of topics, most of which are time wasters and don't help anyone get to a decision. But we can't ignore the buyer completely, and we do have to give them the opportunity for open discussion and debate—so it's best to set up boundaries. In other words, set up the invisible fence to include the topics that matter. Anything outside the fence doesn't matter.

At the end of my presentation, when it's time to decide on next steps, I don't ask for the sale. Instead, I reaffirm my status as an independent expert, and then I set up the invisible fence. How? I teach the buyer how to evaluate whether my deal is right for them. Then, when I'm done, the deal naturally comes together.

1. Introduce the Buyer's Formula

To start, I'll say something like, "I deal with this kind of thing all the time. Let me try and help."

As an example, consider walking into a bike shop looking to get a solid bicycle for some light weekend mountain biking. The bike mechanic who helps you out will say something like, "Look, I've helped a thousand people buy a mountain bike. Let me tell you what I've found works best for a weekend warrior." Statements like "I've done this a thousand times" always reinforce one's status as an independent expert.

2. Outline Obvious Ways to Fail

Next, start to create boundaries that your buyer will not venture outside of, by highlighting the obvious ways to fail.

The bike mechanic might say, "Most amateur athletes who are just getting into trail riding will assume *price* is a way to measure the *quality* of a bike. In reality, higher price just means it's more specialized for one certain type of riding—and useless for others. So don't go by price. And don't buy the frame online because it's a mess out there on the internet: a fifty-four Trek is a fifty-two in Shimano and is a fifty-six in Colnago—nothing matches up from one brand to the next! There are no real standards in this industry like you might have with terabytes for a hard drive, miles per gallon for a car, or percent interest on a loan. With a bike, you sit on it, pedal a few times, and get the *feel* of it. And you have someone like me standing by so you don't make an obvious wrong choice."

3. Highlight Counterintuitive Ways to Fail

From there, you should move on to the less obvious, or counterintuitive, ways to fail. These are traps that most people fall into, things that your buyer surely believes he already knows, but really he doesn't. You are going to expertly point a few of these out and teach your buyer at least one valuable insight.

The mechanic could say, "When you check the bikes out, it's going to seem like carbon fiber and Kevlar are incredibly cool and the right way to go, high tech is best, right? Wrong. Unless you're a pro, those materials are just too fragile. You drop it once, it cracks, and the bike is toast. Sexy materials only benefit riders trying to shave two seconds off a Tour de France time trial. But helmets are exactly the opposite of frames. For helmets, the more expensive they are, the more exotic the material, the safer and higher quality they will be."

Once you've shown your buyer five or six things that can easily go wrong in his decision (starting with the obvious and moving to the less obvious), it's time to shift into the positive actions he can take, so he feels he's in control and is making informed choices.

4. List Obvious Actions

Now you can tell your buyer what actions he should take to get started. Again, start with a few no-brainers, or things your buyer already knows in the back of his mind and will definitely agree with.

"Obviously, you want to remember the bike is only seventy percent of the total cost," the mechanic would continue. "You'll need another six hundred dollars for helmet, pedals, shoes, gloves, and gear, so leave some cash in your pocket. I'd say don't spend more than twenty-five hundred bucks for your first bike—total, for everything, then blow another six hundred on gear."

5. Less Obvious "Hacks"

Then move into the less obvious tips and insights, or the "hacks" (these are the things you would only figure out by doing it at least 100 times).

"What I'd do," the bike mechanic says, "is start with basic Shimano 105 components. They're great, that's what I ride. You won't need anything more than that for now. Get yourself a cheap Trek or Giant frame, all metal, a solid helmet like Giro Vanquish MIPS, and some high-quality shoes—SIDI Defender's will work. Then, if you're going to be riding more than ten miles a week, definitely spend a few bucks on a comfortable seat—go for the Eron, it's bombproof. *Trust me on the seat.* After you get a hundred plus rides in on this bike, sell it and upgrade to XTR components and *then* spend five thousand on something you love that will keep you happy for the next five years."

6. Hand Over Autonomy

Finally, hand over autonomy with a shrug and a line that detaches you from the outcome, like, "Yeah, well, that's just what I'd do, having done it at least a hundred times already. I'm not the boss of you. You can do whatever you want."

If you've done everything right, the buyer will enter a stage of pessimism and will start seriously considering the positives and negatives of your deal and asking questions—but it's more likely those questions will all stay within the boundaries you set up in your Buyer's Formula.

7. Redirect to Keep the Buyer "In Bounds"

From time to time the buyer will venture outside the boundaries you have set and ask about something that you already said was a rookie mistake in your Buyer's Formula. The better you get at delivering the formula, the less often you'll have to field rogue questions, but here's how to deal with them when they do come up.

First, let the buyer fully object. Hear him out, then redirect firmly to stay within the boundaries you previously set. "People are always worried about that issue, and in the end, it's never even an issue at all," the bike mechanic would say. "There are twenty-five different things to worry about when you're buying a bike, but there are really only five things that actually matter. Just focus on these five and everything will be perfect. Get distracted by the other twenty and you'll waste time and money and end up with the wrong thing."

With the formula, the bike shop mechanic has boiled down and shared with you ten years of bike-buying experience. But what if the buyer doesn't want to follow the suggested formula? The answer is simple: He doesn't want to follow an expert's opinion; he's a do-it-yourselfer and thinks he knows everything from a few internet searches, he will be a pain in the butt for the bike shop the whole time, and the shop is going to lose money dealing with him and all the nitpicking, time-wasting concerns, and eventual complaints.

I've seen this a thousand times too. If the buyer won't respect your expert status and your Buyer's Formula, he's never going to be a good customer, partner, or investor. Start backing away from him.

But once your buyer has the Buyer's Formula and does accept your expert status, you have laid an invisible fence. Now you can safely step back and provide autonomy.

As I've said previously, don't beat down every objection or discourage pessimism. Entertain the objections. Welcome the pessimism. Acknowledge the downside of what you offer. Some valid objections will come up in any proposal, and telling your buyer otherwise and shooting down every one of his objections will signal to him that you are being less than authentic, or worse, needy (and difficult to work with).

It's a good idea to bring to the surface the most obvious flaws in your plan before the buyer does, although most people try to avoid any mention of negatives. You should move in quickly and acknowledge the possibility of failure and the obvious negative features—or he will do so but at the most inconvenient time. Do all this and you will gain your buyer's trust. When you embrace pessimism along with the buyer, he won't feel pressured, and he will be the one to say, "Yes, I love it. What's the best way to work together and get started?"

THAT'S HOW THE Buyer's Formula works. It's what I was about to teach Bulletz4Breakfast, the top sniper in the world, in order to recruit him to Zero Gravity's *Counter-Strike* team and carry our deal to its rightful conclusion.

A BUYER'S FORMULA FOR LATE-CAREER ATHLETES

Bulletz was curious about what I had to say. But he was already making a lot of money, was already a sought-after celebrity signature and playing on a good team. He was so good, in fact, he didn't have to compete in the preliminary round because his team was already guaranteed a spot in the finals, which gave him some time to sneak away, meeting me in the hotel café as the first round of the tournament was starting. On our side, Anton was going to try and win the preliminary game without a sniper, keeping the slot open in hopes that we would find someone before the finals. Then we could register whoever we landed in the sniper position as a member of our team before game two.

When we sat down at the conference center Starbucks, Bulletz was barely paying attention, looking around at other small groups to see if there was a better meeting he could bounce out to. I needed a quick Status Tip-Off. "Listen," I said, before he even uttered a word, "let's give this situation a name: You're a late-career athlete. Most late-career athletes melt down in the last year or two. It's pretty sad because their last media appearance is not on ESPN celebrating a big win; it's on TMZ revealing divorce, drugs, and disaster. I've helped late-career athletes avoid the dustbin of history in professional basketball, football, NASCAR, UFC, even surfing. What do you think I'm doing for Anton? How do you think a retired eSports athlete is still making millions of dollars? I put together the business model, tax strategy, marketing funnel, intellectual property licensing, financial controls, balance sheet, and investor base. I'm going to take his company public in the spring and he'll make at least ten million. That situation has a name too—it's called *set for life*."

"How'd he do all that?" Bulletz asked. He was intrigued. These were the exact things he was starting to care about in his own life.

"First thing is, you can't be seen as flipping from being the best sniper in the world to being a *nobody*. I don't ever want to read how the great Bulletz faded away, lost his touch, and imploded. Think about Michael Jordan. Only thing people can remember about his retirement is that he switched to baseball but wasn't very good, then went back to basketball but wasn't very good there either. Or Brett Favre, the superstar Green Bay Packers quarterback, who moved to the Jets and then the Vikings in his last few seasons. Megastar to benchwarmer—it's the wrong way to end an incredible career.

"Right now you have to focus on just a few things that really matter, and ignore everything else," I continued, jumping straight to my Buyer's Formula. "Most important: You don't ever want fans to feel sorry for you, or to pity you. Your name should inspire generations of athletes in every sport to play hard, play fair, and behave like a champion whether winning or losing. Inspiration, not pity—got it?" He nodded. I glanced down at my phone under the table to see how Zero Gravity and the team were doing. Things were absolutely *not* looking good. His men were easy targets without a sniper to provide cover fire.

What I saw on my phone was not making me feel like much of a champion. The mobile app was incredible, and I could see live video of the game play and all the battle specs as easily as I could watch the evening news. Just three minutes into the main battle, our boys were already banged up. They were all low on health and losing ground fast.

I tore myself away from the action and back to the conversation with Bulletz. He looked up from whatever he was doing on his phone to listen for a moment.

"A lot of retired athletes try to reinvent themselves, and switch to a totally new industry, like restaurants, car dealerships, home building, financial services," I continued, "but it almost never works out. What does a retired basketball player, hockey player . . . or *sniper* . . . know about running a car dealership? Nothing. Which is my point. So it begs the question—where do old athletes get work? Yeah, you guessed it. Joe Namath put his name on Beautymist Pantyhose. That's a true story. A better example, John Madden, video games; Tony Hawk, toy skateboards. But those are the lucky ones. Because if we're being frank with each other, you aren't John Madden or Tony Hawk. Most retired athletes end up doing color commentary for the local news on high school football or endorsing some shady bail bond company. So the rule here is, stick with what you know—no reinventing yourself; that is too risky. For you, it means you're in eSports for the rest of your life. And why not? You *love* the game and you would be miserable selling salad dressing."

"Yeah, I love the game. But how can I do that?" he asked. His body language was open and he had a thoughtful expression on his face, so I decided to stop focusing on the list of don'ts and instead push forward and reveal the positives, the things he could actually do.

"Well, obviously you want to announce your retirement in advance, so it doesn't look like you're desperate. It's a planned retirement. You are going out on top, *on your own terms*. And you also want to announce your new position in the eSports industry. But here's the important piece: In what capacity? Announcer? Coach? Those jobs are second-string and pay next to nothing. You want to become a team owner. This lets you own something that will grow in value. This way you'll have leverage in the future. That's why I was so excited to share this deal with you. Because Anton wants you as a sniper now, but he also sees you as a partner and on the team for years and years. This is the only chance to negotiate hard. Come back in a few years after you've washed out—you'll find out there are no offers out there for has-beens and bail bond salesmen."

The boundaries were set. It was time to invite pessimism.

Otherwise it would just creep in later when I wasn't around to assist in the decision making.

"Anyway," I said, shrugging, "that's just what I would suggest after working with many other athletes in your position. But everyone's career is different, and there are some very real risks to switching teams while you're still active in the game. I absolutely understand that. I'm not the boss of you and can't tell you what to do. *Only you can decide what's right.*" And then I stopped talking.

For a few painful moments, neither of us said a word. Bulletz was deep in thought. He looked back at his phone and I thought to myself, "These darn millennials are always distracted by something!" Then suddenly he jumped up, excusing himself for a moment to use the restroom. They also have small bladders.

While he was gone, I pulled out my phone again to check on the raging battle between Anton and the insurgents. The situation was worse than before. The video feed showed our machine gunner, Smith, lying prone in the courtyard, totally exposed to whoever was shooting at him. Bullets sparked all around him. But the kid was an iceberg. Ignoring the incoming 9 mm rounds, he shouldered his M249 squad automatic weapon (SAW) and tore off a blistering burst of return fire.

I could see on the screen that Anton peeked around the wall into the courtyard where the main fighting was taking place. "Give me another weapon system!" he screamed in frustration. "I need another 240 SAW!" Unable to see the enemy, Anton was going to die if he stayed in that doorway.

Outside, in the courtyard, Smith was hit and he *did* die.

Dammit, he hadn't taken down a single enemy! His screen turned to digital snow and he was out. It was the same story for Brown, Davis, and Miller, all out of the fight.

This was the end of the road for our squad. We were pinned down, surrounded, and left with no other option than to jump into the narrow courtyard and face the firepower of their enemy's tripod-mounted PKM and AK-47s head-on. We wouldn't have much of a chance to survive that kind of firepower, but it was the only move we had.

A full five minutes had passed in game time. Anton "Zero Gravity" was out front, taking fire and low on health. Cooper, Murphy, and Jenkins were low on ammo. Just then, a string of 7.62 x 54 mm tracer rounds were blasting from above into the already chaotic firefight, blowing out the glass; someone was pouring high-caliber suppressing fire straight onto the other team's position. Suppressing fire is the good kind of shooting that goes past you, straight into the enemy, pinning them down, and gives you a chance to move around. Suddenly, it was the other side, the red team, who was in trouble. Whoever was shooting from behind us had our enemies scrambling, abandoning their positions, ducking for cover. Two red team members went down in a splatter, and now . . . four were down. What the . . . ? For the moment, our enemies stopped firing at us. This was our chance to get out of the kill zone. Anton and team made a break into the courtyard and started unloading everything we had in the enemy's direction. Now five of red team were down. Another one killed by our team made six. On our side, Anton was hit as he scrambled through the courtyard, but still alive.

A blizzard of metal and glass fragments exploded next to the last red team insurgent, who was running for cover, and I followed the red tracer fire backward to its point of origin on the screen. Behind Anton, about two hundred feet back, up on a neighboring rooftop, I could now make out the form of a sniper barrel clicking off high-impact 7.62 rounds and taking out the red team insurgents methodically, accurately, with one impossible shot after the next.

At that moment I knew we were going to make it to the next round in the tournament and probably win the whole thing—Bulletz had joined the fight, and the team.

CHAPTER 7

How to Be Compelling

I love speed. Speed is a lifestyle. Cars, trucks, motorcycles, you name it—there's something profound and thrilling about being so close to a road, pushing the man-machine limit. I've blazed through back roads and open roads, fast lanes and country lanes, lonesome roads, happy trails, and highways to hell. By the time I was in my late twenties, I'd stockpiled Porsches, muscle cars, and about fifty motorcycles. Cars are good. Motorcycles are better.

Nearly all my motorcycles came from the same dealer—Elias, the coolest ride captain who ever carved a canyon. Elias didn't just sell motorcycles, he *was* motorcycles. From his all-Japan racing jacket to his series of smoking hot girlfriends covered in anime tattoos to his twenty-mile stare that pierced through any roadblock, Elias screamed speed. He graduated from the University of

Motorcycles and he just looks fast, even when he's standing still. But more than being good-looking and popular, below the surface he's imaginative, perceptive, and two steps ahead of everyone else. A guy like this was irresistible to an axle addict like me.

Elias had a hardscrabble upbringing in San Jose, California. He owed his mastery of motorcycles to an errant childhood and an insightful cop who urged him to ease his adolescent angst on the racetrack. He was fast and when it came to winning a race, he was the real deal.

He owned a successful boutique motorcycle dealership in West Hollywood, which was, like him, the height of cool. You needed to be a millionaire to get in the door. To get back out, you'd leave with a lot less. I loved hanging out with Elias and his posse, drinking tequila and talking bikes. We'd go out for sushi, and except for me, everybody looked like the bass player from Scorpions—especially the actual Scorpions bass player, who would join us whenever he was in town. The guest roster included Gucci models, Nicolas Cage, and world champion racer John Kocinski, and I was the finance guy (read: the nerd who paid for everyone's drinks). Just to fit in and hang out with these dudes, I bought the actual Camaro from the Metallica video for "I Disappear." But still, they'd all shake their heads, point to me, and ask Elias, "Who's the suit?" Even with ripped jeans and a 1968 Camaro, I looked corporate.

I may have been utterly uncool next to these guys but I didn't mind. I was just happy and grateful to be invited into the real Hollywood Hills and its loud, exciting, reckless world of motorcycle racers, models, and rock stars. I was riding high. It was over one of these sushi dinners that Elias and I started talking about going into business together.

"I'd like to scale the business," he said with his characteristic unaffected directness. "I was thinking about starting an apparel line. You know, Hollywood Hills meets Formula 1. Von Dutch for speed. A true speed lifestyle company. What do you say, Oren? Let's do this together and have some fun."

"Of course. I'd love to," I said breathlessly, because that's just what happens if you're a guy like me being offered the opportunity to go into the speed business with a titanium piston god.

Elias ended up being a piston god who could *sell like a demon.* What a natural. Our company never had sales meetings or pipeline reports, and we never gave a thought to any kind of sales methods because, well, we had the Elias method. He knew everything about speed. Ferrari street special? Ducati race bike? Porsche Le Mans winner? He could tell you what it was worth and why, and follow up with two stories about it, one involving some wild engineering facts and the other involving two alcohol-fueled nights in the seedy part of Monte Carlo. Elias's stories sold vehicles, and these sales were worth millions to our business.

As fantastic as the stories were, you never questioned them, because they were also grounded in fascinating facts. Elias had a vast working knowledge of his industry and his products, which he bought and sold like pieces of art. And he wouldn't sell to just anybody. If you wanted to buy a motorcycle from him—or a motorcycle part, for that matter—you had to convince him to sell it to you.

But in order to generate the extra revenue we needed to get the apparel line off the ground, Elias and I determined that we'd have to dramatically ramp up the number of motorcycles we were selling. Until now, his business model had been simple: Import exotic motorcycles from Italy and Japan and sell them to rich guys in Beverly Hills. Through Elias's reputation and personal magnetism, sales happened like magic.

Now that we were in business together, I had to figure out how to scale our operations to meet our new sales targets. We needed to sell our motorcycles to buyers beyond Beverly Hills, in a way that wasn't dependent on Elias's natural in-person sales talent. In order to ship faster to both coasts, we decided to open our next facility in Devils Lake, North Dakota. Elias had gotten a killer deal on this warehouse out there, but of course he couldn't leave Beverly Hills because we needed him to sell the fancy bikes that supported the whole operation. And there was no way I was moving to North Dakota because, well, I was doing just fine, living on Sunset Boulevard, one block from the Whisky a Go Go.

So we had to hire a local North Dakota sales staff—and that's where our problems started. We needed to figure out how to teach our people from North Dakota to sell like Elias. We had to make them compelling. This meant I was headed to Devil's Lake to train the team.

My task? Turn this frozen warehouse in the middle of the country into a high-powered sales office for Italian auto parts. "No problem," I thought to myself smugly. "What could possibly go wrong?" At that point in my career, I'd sold everything from accounting software to brain aneurysm coils. I'd launched a genetic data company, I could explain in detail how to inject your knee with ortho-guided synovial fluid, and I could chart the subdomains on the dark web where stolen financial data is stored.

So seriously, how hard could it possibly be to sell a few Ducati parts?

As I was about to discover, it was pretty damn hard, because, it turned out, if Elias was the living embodiment of sexiness and speed, this North Dakota sales team was the embodiment of . . . ice.

REVERSE ENGINEERING THE ART
OF COMPELLINGNESS

What does it even mean to be *compelled*? In its most basic form, it's that feeling of being unable to look away from something or someone. It can feel like being caught in a trance or placed under a spell, and it can lead you to a sudden insight in a way that opens the door to Inception. But what is it that actually makes one person more compelling than another?

Sure, most of us can easily recognize the basics of a compelling individual: a winning smile, a great sense of humor, an attractive physique, a keen intelligence. Personal charisma is a patchwork of complex and sophisticated social and emotional skills that allow charismatic individuals to affect and influence others without pushing, forcing, or even persuading.

I used to think a compelling person was made up of three

elements: appearance, intelligence, and enthusiasm. And then I tried backing this up with research, only to find that, while those traits certainly make someone likable, enthusiasm doesn't contribute to compellingness *at all*, and it can even cause salespeople to inadvertently scare away customers.

If enthusiasm isn't the secret to compellingness, then maybe it's sex appeal.

No, it's not that either. My research quickly revealed that physical attractiveness isn't going to move the needle very far in business, politics, or dealmaking. Kim Jong Un, for instance, is decidedly not sexy by our Western standards. You'd have to search far into some weird subcultures to find someone who wants to swipe right for Mr. Un. Despite that, with his finger over the nuke launch button, he is incredibly *compelling* and a regular feature at the top of the news cycle.

But what about intelligence? That was the last element I looked at, and I was sure it would hold the key. Surely smarter people would be seen as more competent and trustworthy and this would lead others to find them more compelling. But did this theory hold up to research? Not at all. In fact, the smartest people in the world can often put you to sleep the fastest.

Take Harry Markopolos, a brilliant quantitative financial specialist with an instinct for the numbers behind complex derivatives. He smelled a rat in the workings of Bernie Madoff Investment Securities as far back as 1999, spotting Madoff's $65 billion Ponzi scheme years before it came to light. Markopolos lived in fear for his life, spending everything he had trying to convince the world (and the Securities and Exchange Commission) the fraud actually existed. He contacted politicians and badgered journalists to write about Madoff. He even presented the SEC with a detailed dossier in 2005 bluntly titled "The World's Largest Hedge Fund Is a Fraud."

So why didn't anyone pay attention?

Markopolos should have been extremely compelling to the government, the media, and other investment funds: He was intelligent, had the story of the century, and was screaming through a giant megaphone. Still, nobody found him worth paying much attention to. He wasn't able to get his idea across when it mattered most. Though he's brilliant and well-spoken, he lacked something.

So what sets aside the most compelling people from the rest of us who are "merely" likable, smart, and enthusiastic? It seems impossible to pin down something specific that the rest of us could copy. We can't all be movie stars, win the Super Bowl, or control a nuclear missile site. I combed through the data and research articles and conducted interviews, but it seemed there was no one who had really tackled this to my satisfaction. So I kept at it, looking for a replicable formula.

And then I had a breakthrough. I eventually figured out how to be compelling by first figuring out how *not* to be compelling.

Over the years, I've boiled all my research down into a method to skyrocket your ability to be compelling. Unfortunately, I hadn't discovered any of this yet when I woke up flat on my back on a sheet of ice in Devils Lake, North Dakota.

MEETING THE TEAM—AT 20 BELOW

I could not feel my left leg. A searing pain was pressing into my neck. My right arm was numb and my ears were ringing. I turned to the side and slowly opened my eyes. The snow was turning to reddish-brown slush under my head. "I must be bleeding," I thought, trying to remember what had just happened.

If you had to pick a place on the map that was the exact polar—and I do mean *polar*—opposite of my home in Beverly Hills, there's a good chance you'd choose Devils Lake.

First of all, it's always cold there, unless it's blisteringly hot. Today it was minus 20.

A thermal glove materialized in front of my eyes. "Here, boss," said Big Danny, the lead supervisor of the warehouse. "Take my hand. You stay down any longer, your head's gonna freeze to the pavement. Probably have to cut your hair to get you up then. I've seen it happen."

"Wait," I said through chattering teeth, trying to piece together the past few minutes. "I think I'm bleeding. Maybe don't move me." Was I going into shock from blood loss? Was I going to die, here, in the parking lot of the Dew Drop Inn?

"That's not blood, chief; that's the coffee you spilled. You're fine; let's get moving."

Danny didn't wait for me to get up on my own; he bent down, pulled me up by the front of my jacket, and brushed me off like I was five. I struggled to regain my balance, noticing that the parking lot of my motel was on a steep, icy hill. I had just fallen while standing on a literal slippery slope (I was starting to understand why they warn you about those).

At least I wasn't burned by my full cup of steaming hot coffee as I went down—it froze in midair on the way to my face. On that particular day in January it was so cold you couldn't even get chocolate—they told me the stuff just explodes into ice crystals at -35 degrees, so they don't carry it until May at the earliest.

"You're gonna need to get some real boots out here," Big Danny told me, stating the obvious. He looked me over and clearly didn't find me very impressive. "And you should get a puffier coat and a warm hat that covers your ears. Remember, out here the native Inuits still use refrigerators so they can keep their food from freezing. You get that, boss? It's so cold you need a fridge to keep your food from turning into ice vapor . . . and, you know, just to educate you on some key survival strategies up here, you lose eighty percent of your body heat through your head. Can't afford to do that in North Dakota, no sir. You want me to take you to the Walmart before we head to the shop and get you rigged out?"

"Ah, no thanks, Big Danny," I said, limping toward his truck. "I don't want to be late on my first day meeting the team."

"Your funeral," he said with a shrug.

I climbed into the passenger's side of his truck, anxious to get into the heated cab. Except it was freezing inside the truck too.

Big Danny eased onto Highway 20, one of the only two major arteries going through town. He pointed off into the distance, where I could just make out a Walmart sign.

"Are you sure you don't want to stop off, boss? It'll only take a minute and you'll be a whole lot more comfortable. No offense, but dressing like that up here, they're going to think you're stupid or crazy or both."

I had never been to a Walmart. Through chattering teeth I answered, *"Yes please, Walmart."*

In the store, I quickly grabbed some insulated boots, a workman's coat, a pair of leather construction gloves, and a hat that Big Danny insisted I buy (even though it looked ridiculous on me).

"Great hat," Dawn, our cashier, said cheerfully as she rang us up. "I bought that same one for my husband last year." Danny smiled at me and pointed at Dawn, nodding his head. "You going to wear them boots out?" Dawn trained her eyes on me. She was intense and seemed to be letting me know that she'd just made a very helpful suggestion. I changed my boots right there in front of her, embarrassed by my colorful but out-of-place Fred Segal socks.

I glanced up at Dawn and, sure enough, she was eyeballing my socks with the trained eye of a cold weather survivalist. It suddenly occurred to me that I might have a little culture clash problem with the sales team I was about to meet. I was going to be walking into a room full of Dannys and Dawns and trying to command their respect and loyalty. Maybe this was going to be harder than I originally thought.

Devils Lake, I realized, was not the kind of place where locals used phrases like "emotionally charged imagery" or "dramatic character arc" or "protagonist-driven plot"—concepts that were the norm back home in Hollywood. How was I going to turn the staff of this town into a team of compelling salespeople?

I had two days with the team before I had to head to New York for another deal. That gave me about forty-eight hours to figure out how to teach Big Danny and Little Danny, Gus "Guzzler" Gussard, Tommy no-last-name, Tiffany, and her daughter Crystal how to sell motorcycles like Elias, legendary motorcycle and Jet Ski racer, airplane racer, and Hollywood Hills rock-and-roll tequila-drinking go-all-nighter.

As we pulled up in front of the shop a few minutes later, I was getting the jitters. What was I going to tell these people that they would understand and be able to use to improve sales? What could they possibly have in common with a guy like Elias?

I stepped into the company office, ready to teach them what I knew. But the first thing I noticed was that it was freezing cold inside. Nobody was wearing a coat. They acted as if it was 72 degrees or something.

"What's the temperature in here?" I asked.

"Fifty-five," said Little Danny, Big Danny's assistant. "If you want something warm, I can make you a cup of coffee in the microwave."

Microwave coffee? *No thanks.*

I headed straight to the back of the freezing warehouse, where the whole team had assembled to hear me speak. I stepped onto the makeshift stage—a piece of plywood perched atop four paint buckets. The howling wind was banging a drum solo against the corrugated tin walls.

I could tell by their faces that I didn't look like anything the Dannys, or Crystal, or Gus, or Tommy, or Tiffany had ever seen before. Despite Big Danny's best efforts to dress me as a local with boots and my puffy coat and my ridiculous hat, I looked like the Man Who Fell to Earth.

I laid it all out for them. "Despite our best intentions, we're only selling about seventy-five thousand dollars a week, not nearly enough. This puts our whole company into negative territory, and there's frustration at the home office. That's why I'm here today, to help kick things into gear. I've been doing this a long time, and here's how I like to think about our business: Nobody *needs* an Italian racing motorcycle. Ducati, Guzzi, whatever . . . Compare our customer to a shopper in your local Walmart—he is buying stuff he *needs*: a snowplow, a generator, a block heater, a jumper cable. But our products are different. Our products serve an emotional purpose. It's about *desire*, not *necessity*. It's about the opportunity to spend some money needlessly on a desire. So your job is to increase that desire. And how do you do that? By making our products harder to buy."

Blank faces. I couldn't tell if I had blown their minds or if they were just waiting for me to leave.

"So . . . are there any questions on that?" I asked.

Little Danny raised his hand.

"Yeah, go ahead, Little Danny."

"What's a Guzzi?"

"Danny, it's a European motorcycle that we sell parts for. C'mon, man, that's what we *do here*. But listen, the point is, you guys are making the sale too easy for the buyer and it's killing your deals. Neediness! Discounts! Stop doing all that stuff. Make the customer fight for it. Make these products hard to attain, while simultaneously feeding the customer's desire for them."

Crystal's hand went up. "So what you're saying is that we need to try and not sell people things so that they'll try harder to spend their money on things they don't need."

"That's right!" I said, delighted that I'd reached at least one member of the team.

"I don't get it," she said.

Oh man, I was so out of my element.

"OK, guys," I said, clapping my hands together, "that's probably enough instruction for now. Why don't you get out there and make some calls? I'll be listening in to see what you might be doing right or wrong. Then, tomorrow, we can have another meeting like this. Great work, team!"

And without waiting for acknowledgment, I hopped off the "stage" and headed straight to my "office," letting it be known that anyone who wanted to come ask questions was welcome.

Nobody came.

Oh well. I easily spotted my office along the side of the warehouse. It was the rusted metal door with "Oren's Office" written on a Post-it note with a smiley face. I pushed through the door, wincing at the cold. My eyes immediately went to the tiny space heater in the corner; it was silent, unplugged. There was another Post-it note on it: "This works." For the first time since arriving in Devils Lake, I burst into a huge smile.

Then I buckled down and got to work.

I fired up my computer and pressed Play on our sales-management software, which recorded all our calls. It was Gus talking to a UK motorcycle enthusiast. The buyer was looking for a new set of front forks for his Ducati Superleggera and we were one of the few vendors who carried it. "Nice," I thought to myself, "here's twelve thousand dollars in the bag before it even started."

Except it wasn't.

Gus scared the client away and the call ended awkwardly: "So what do you think? I can get these shipped out to you tomorrow, be there by Tuesday—do you want to pay by credit card, or . . ." Same thing on the next call with Tiffany and a guy from New York who needed a gas tank for his Moto Guzzi MGS-01. And the one after that between Tommy and a buyer in Arkansas looking for a set of carbon fiber wheels.

As the tapes rolled and the heater fan whirred quietly, I stripped off one layer of clothing at a time. My down jacket. My windbreaker. My thermal hooded sweatshirt. Eventually my wool hat. The tapes of sales calls kept rolling, one after another, as I paced around the office, thinking. There was something similar happening on every single call, a roadblock that our sales team was hitting. It was weird because we weren't that bad. We were polite. We asked questions. We gave detailed product descriptions. We explained why this product was better than that product. We tried to explain away objections. We asked for the order a few times. Isn't that what salespeople do? It didn't matter which of our salespeople it was or where the buyer was located or what they were trying to purchase—the result was the same. The call ended awkwardly with the buyer making excuses and deferring the decision to later, because he had to "check in" with an unavailable partner or mechanic or wife or brother or a few Teletubbies, or whoever, and then quickly getting off the phone—presumably to go search the internet for a better deal.

But I couldn't put my finger on exactly what it was the sales team was doing wrong. Sure, they could have been more charismatic, or given more technical information, or been less needy, but there was something *big* going on here.

After six hours straight at my desk, I was fried and I didn't have a definitive answer. I stopped the tapes and leaned back in my chair, thinking. And for some reason, my eyes fell on the mini–basketball hoop in the corner of the office.

"Yes," I thought to myself, "of course. *That's it!*"

Just then, a phone rang. Apparently I had an office line. I found an old-school Panasonic cordless phone in the desk drawer and picked it up. "This is Oren," I said a little hesitantly. Nobody knew where I was. And anyone who did would not be calling me with good news.

"Hi Oren, it's Elias. Listen, got a call from Danny today. He's worried about what you're doing up there. The team doesn't like you that much. He says they're ready to dump you into the lake first chance they get to make it look like an accident. I guess we're going to have to pull you out of there and try something else." He sounded disappointed.

"Hey, I don't want to be argumentative, but the problem is *you*, not me," I said. "Elias, you're too good—ten people here doesn't equal one of you. You are a natural-born salesman. You were literally born to sell anything on wheels. Girls love you. Guys love you. Hell, *I* love you. Compellingness is in your DNA. You instinctively understand how to create beauty, allure, exclusivity, and desire. You know how to sell power and speed, to create an irresistible appeal. For you, things just sell themselves.

"I've been listening to tapes of their calls all day and I realized something," I continued. "These guys have been trying to follow what you do, but it's not working for them because they aren't you."

I threw the basketball to the mini-hoop and it bounced off the rim. I was never a good shot anyway.

"It's like . . . Remember that scene in *White Men Can't Jump*?"

I heard a laugh on the other end of the line because we had watched the movie together at least five times.

"That scene where Wesley Snipes and Woody Harrelson beat this guy Raymond in a five-hundred-dollar winner-take-all pickup game, so Raymond needs more money to keep playing, he gets a gun from his car, walks to the corner liquor store, puts on a ski mask, points that forty-five Magnum at the store owner," I said. "Remember what the store owner says?"

"Yeah, of course," said Elias, as he quotes the line from the movie. "'Raymond, is that you? Take that damn mask off!'"

"Exactly!" I was getting to the point now. "And right after he's recognized by the shopkeeper, Raymond pulls off the ski mask, drops the whole gangster persona, and goes back to being his normal self. He reminds the shopkeeper that he should be protecting his store better because it's a dangerous neighborhood. Then Raymond sells his gun to the shopkeeper at a good price in a quick negotiation, everyone's happy, and Raymond gets the cash he needs to keep playing basketball against Wesley Snipes."

I made my final point: "When Raymond tried to pose as someone he's not, even with the ski mask, it was obvious. The shopkeeper sees right through it. But when Raymond drops the phony stuff and just acts like his normal self, a wheeler-dealer, he gets the deal done."

I explained how we were making the same mistake in our office by wearing different masks during the sales calls and trying to take on personalities that were not our own. "When I listened to those sales calls today," I said to Elias, "I looked at it from the customer's point of view. To the customer, our staff has so many different personalities, it's sort of a multiple personality disorder. Our salesperson doesn't feel authentic or real. We're trying too hard. I think I can fix this problem."

THE FIVE PERSONALITIES OF
THE SALES APOCALYPSE

What I had realized in Devils Lake is that the salespeople on our team, much like salespeople everywhere, were struggling to make sales by using a loser's formula. During nearly every sales call, they shifted from persona to persona, appealing to whatever emotional state the buyer was in at that moment. It boiled down to five different personas, or archetypes. This change from persona to persona confuses buyers, who crave consistency and certainty from people they're doing business with. These are the five personas that make up the Loser's Formula, listed in order of their appearance in most sales presentations:

1. The Ultimate Nice Guy
2. The ShamWow Guy
3. The Sorcerer
4. The Angel
5. The Wolf

I'll break these down in a bit more detail.

1. The Ultimate Nice Guy

At the top of a sales call, most people start by putting on the Ultimate Nice Guy persona. In other words, we play it safe. We want above all else to be liked, and we try to achieve this by seeking common ground. *Great to talk to you today! Where are you calling from? Really, my uncle used to live in Houston, hot down there in the summer. Plans for the weekend? Fishing! I love fishing, my grandfather used to . . .* Then, shifting to work topics, it goes a little like this: *What kind of business are you in? Oh, that's awesome, I love pest control!* The Ultimate Nice Guy is the first archetype or mask that salespeople fall into because it is the easiest and safest approach. No one is going to complain about a pleasant, approach-able, friendly start to a call. This leads to surface-level conversa-tion: current news, weather, sports, empty exchanges.

What's wrong with a nice guy? At a basic level, nothing, and it's certainly true people are more likely to do business with us if they like us. Look, I get it—the impulse at the top of the meeting is to impress upon others we are nice and relatable and have common ground with the buyer. But the real problem with the Ultimate Nice Guy persona is that it signals to the buyer how much power he has over us. Once we have lost status (and given away our power) we shift from the Ultimate Nice Guy archetype into the ShamWow Guy archetype, who will go on to explain all the fea-tures of the product or idea.

2. The ShamWow Guy

People expect to know what it is we're selling, right? So we start listing the best features of the product, our most famous custom-ers, the five-star ratings, our incredible customer service reputa-tion, and our recent industry awards. This is where we become the ShamWow Guy.

For those who haven't seen the ShamWow commercials, here's some background:

Over three weekends in the summer of 2007, Israeli-born film-maker and entrepreneur Offer Shlomi shot a two-minute com-mercial extolling the virtues of the ShamWow, a cleaning towel that promised to soak up twelve times its weight in spilled liquids and revolutionize your life. Shlomi handled the yellow cloth with the dexterity of a stage magician, wiping up small puddles and blotting soda-soaked carpets, describing an endless list of features for what was basically a thirty-five-cent kitchen cloth. Nobody was better than Shlomi at hyping features.

When we're in the ShamWow archetype, we similarly spring into action listing everything our product can do, has done, and might do in the future. It has a hundred terabytes; we are the only ones with hyper-threading; we're FINRA compliant; we can do it in four weeks when everyone else takes six weeks or longer. *Oh, and did I mention it comes with free shipping, a 15 percent discount, and a money-back guarantee?*

Of course, this information overload usually doesn't get through to the buyer unless he already has idea receptors built for whatever we're trying to tell him. Once all the best and brightest features and facts of the product are out on the table we realize, *Yikes! I need to explain how these features will actually benefit the buyer.* And then, yet another transformation begins.

3. The Sorcerer

The Juiceman juicer was one of the first products to be sold and brands built through the infomercial format. The Juiceman show featured energetic pitchman Jay Kordich, who blends an orange, a carrot, and some parsley, then goes on to explain how *fantastic* the rest of your life will be once you're able to do this in your own kitchen. You'll soon be smarter, more handsome, and more attractive to both men and women. After buying this product, you'll date and marry the person of your dreams, who is also smart, ravishing, athletic, and rich. You'll have beautiful children together who will be good at math, play polo with the Rockefeller kids, win national chess competitions, attend Harvard, invent a cryptocurrency, and buy you a retirement mansion in Malibu.

The Sorcerer archetype explains how each of the product's amazing features will benefit the buyer in many exciting (but unverifiable) ways. He or she spins the features into a set of magical benefits. Depending on individual personality, there may be a little sleight of hand here with the numbers, some showmanship with a demonstration, and possibly the sharing of "secrets." ("You didn't hear it from me, but this is the same software Jerry Seinfeld uses to keep track of his ninety-seven Porsches.") The Sorcerer mask will stay on until the buyer is sold on how great life will be after going into business with us.

4. The Angel

Now that we've given the buyer all the information he ever wanted (and never wanted) about our products and ideas, and we've tried to get him super excited about the benefits our products offer, we really need to know the chances of closing the deal—high or low, good or bad? Now it feels time to do a "trial close" and see how close or far we really are to making some money. Who better to test the waters without causing a ripple in the pond than the Angel persona? She is a sweet, kind cherub who looks and sounds easy-going, wonderful to work with, submissive, and eager to please as she asks, "So what do you think? Is this something you'd be interested in? Any questions before we move forward?"

By this time in the sale, the buyer has been talking to just one person, but he's encountered four different characters, each of them formulaic and unimaginative, each completely self-serving and predictable. It's off-putting and the buyer starts to wonder, "Who are you really? What are your values, what do you stand for, and how far will you go just to make the deal?"

The buyer's caution grows as time goes on, even as he is controlling the sale and owning the relationship. He will decide what happens next, how fast things will progress, and ultimately what the final price will be—if a deal is even to be made. But first, he will respond to the Angel's trial close by introducing objections, himself testing the waters for discounts, free upgrades, and other signs of weakness.

The buyer offers, "Well, you know, it'd be really hard for us to switch accounting software so late in the year; we haven't fully budgeted for this kind of expense. It's good to know what our options are." The Angel has done little but push the buyer to voice a full range of objections. As the Angel is overwhelmed, these objections must be overcome, and the final transformation takes shape.

5. The Wolf

Things are getting hairy, and the final sales archetype now emerges. With the first glimmer of an objection, like the first rays of moonlight falling on a man with the werewolf curse, the Angel rapidly transforms into the Wolf. The Wolf jumps on the buyer's objections to wrangle him into submission and make the objections irrelevant in hopes each one will be dropped, clearing the way to a sale. In practice, the dramatic switch from the Angel to the Wolf is a shock to the buyer, who doesn't know how to respond. He clearly does not enjoy dealing with the Wolf archetype because we have suddenly turned combative and aggressive, but what is even more off-putting is that by this point in the call or presentation, we have taken on the personality of five very different characters. The long-suffering buyer is tired, and doesn't have much energy left for thoughtful debate and considering purchasing options. He either agrees to buy knowing he will drop out later, or pumps the brakes, explaining that no decision can be made until his partner reviews the proposal. (We have not heard of this partner or "committee" previously because they may not even exist.)

KNOWING WE DEFAULT to these five archetypes in the course of a sale, I have long wondered why. Why do we move through these dramatically different personas as we try to sell someone a product, service, or idea?

The cognitive psychologists on my payroll have explained it this way: The human brain is programmed to respond to the immediate demands of any social situation and modify our behavior accordingly. The demands of any presentation push us naturally into a pattern of behavior, virtually every time the same. So as our behavior adapts to what the buyer wants to hear, the classic archetypes of Ultimate Nice Guy, ShamWow guy, Sorcerer, Angel, and Wolf appear in response. While each archetype serves the immediate purpose, the summary effect is negative.

In the final analysis, the buyer concludes, "This guy has multiple personalities!" The problem is, the human brain is built to seek out relationships that offer consistency in character. We desperately want to build a matrix of reliable and predictable social relationships, because we have a deep desire to feel like we understand and control our world and can predict who will do what, and when.

With the typical sales script, however, it's impossible for the buyer to form a consistent mental model of the real you because of the personality changes through five different archetypes. It's easy to imagine how this kind of wearing of masks triggers alarm bells, leading the buyer to conclude that something is wrong here—"This salesperson keeps changing who he really is to chase the sale. And who will he become after I give him the money or agreement? I'm not sure I've seen that character yet, or that I want to."

The solution, of course, is to stop modulating behavior as you move through a presentation. But what, exactly, should you replace it with? By studying Elias and dozens of other naturals in the art of compellingness, I've discovered the answer lies in flipping the script.

MY TWO-DAY TRAINING IN COMPELLINGNESS

The training I delivered to our North Dakota sales team after I had realized what was really going on was a long, cold, yet productive two days. At one point, I even accepted a cup of microwave coffee (and regret having done so to this day). But the results were exactly what we wanted: a huge bump in sales revenue.

So what did I possibly teach in two days that made such a huge difference? A principle called "I'm not always right, but never uncertain."

On day one, I taught the team about Stick to Your Guns Theory, an idea that goes far beyond the trope of self-confidence. In fact, self-assurance is a tired and worn-out concept you'll find in chapter one of every old-fashioned sales manual, and basically what they teach salespeople at "win friends" seminars. Stick to Your Guns, by contrast, has the beating heart of a much bigger idea, the kind that wins wars, changes history, and gives rise to leaders who are talked about for a thousand years: how to have an unshakable set of values and moral boundaries that are always on display to the buyer and at the same time completely immovable. I explained it like this:

Imagine a movie studio called this office, saying they wanted to spend one hundred fifty thousand dollars on a prop bike for Johnny Depp to ride off a cliff in an upcoming bank robbery–style film shoot. And the prop bike they want is a 1968 Moto

Guzzi V7R. If Danny here answered the phone, or if any of you took that call, you would say, "Great. Where do you want us to deliver it?" and you'd fill out the paperwork, take the order, and book the sale.

Not Elias.

Elias would say, "Hold on there, chief—did you say ride a V7R off a cliff? I do not have to tell you the V7R is a holy grail motorcycle; there are just seventeen left in the world—ten of those are in museums . . . and yes, sure I can get one. But to drive one into the ocean, are you completely high on quaaludes? Lose my number." Click.

In fact, this actually happened; the story is legendary among our customers. Paramount Studios had called looking for a period-accurate Moto Guzzi V7R, and Elias told them to go fly a kite, but not exactly in those words. Elias sells some of the most exotic, coveted, cherished vehicles of the modern era. He doesn't burn museum pieces to the ground to make a few bucks. Customers love the fact that he has the integrity not to sell out to the studios, or anyone with a bad attitude, a bad business plan, or a bad reputation. Elias has a fixed set of principles. Now, for sure, they may not be in alignment with the Beverly Hills Police Department, the Catholic Church of West Hollywood, Interpol, Parents Against Rock and Roll, or your grandmother's knitting club, but they are a complete set of principles, easy to understand, based on simple logic, and most important, they don't change from moment to moment, day to day, or year to year. He sticks to his guns, *no matter what.*

I taught our sales team about the Five Personalities of the Sales Apocalypse. The key isn't to try to act how Elias would or how Oren would. The key is to stop being reactive to the needs of the buyer, and write personal scripts that are authentic to who you are, then stick to your guns (politely) anytime a buyer offers resistance or tries to push you around. Discount? *No, not on your life.* Free upgrade? *No, why would I do that?* Send me a proposal? *OK, so we have a verbal agreement on terms?* This prevents the buyer from unmasking you, discrediting you, or changing the script in any way. The only thing he can do is work with you or go away— which sometimes is for the best.

On day two of the training, there were lots of questions. For example, asked Danny, "If I'm not the Ultimate Nice Guy, then what am I?" The answer to this is as easy as it is straightforward: You are the expert. You must become an undisputed expert in the mind of the buyer in the first few minutes, and then continue to add credibility, insight, and competence to this expert status throughout the conversation. The Status Tip-Off and the Flash Roll are the perfect points of entry to creating this expert status. Your own industry knowledge, principles, and experience will cement that status.

In Devils Lake, sales more than doubled the following quarter— and doubled again the quarter after that. The team was soon selling bikes and parts on pace with Elias, and we had learned how to be compelling.

CHAPTER 8

Flip the Script, Go Anywhere, Try Anything, and Put It All on the Line to Win an Impossible Deal

How to Put All the Scripts to Work

Allll kinds of good news arrives to you via text message, without much emotion or ceremony, something like "we had a baby" or "we got the deal," and you might even get a smiley face to go along with it. But bad news is something completely different because it's usually delivered by a phone and in a serious tone. The other side really wants you to feel the pain they are feeling. This is why Simon's taut tone telegraphed the bad news as soon as I picked up the phone. "Oren, old boy," he said with a stiff British accent. "It seems we've gone pear shaped on a deal, and I never thought I'd be in this position, but I'm going to call in a favor you owe me." He continued with the details: "We buggered up an important client, Volka Motors UK. Now the account is being awarded to *Bradford-McCoy* in New York next week." I could hear bits of spit fly from his lips as he said the words *Bradford-McCoy*, the agency he'd left twelve years ago to start his own firm. "We've popped our clogs—it's bad news to lose a UK account to a bunch of . . . Americans."

"Yeah, how embarrassing," I said, rolling my eyes as I sat in my office in California. But I couldn't fault him for being so anxious. This was indeed very bad news for Simon, who was CEO of one of the hippest ad agencies in London. Simon is the kind of charming, tall, blue-eyed, square-jawed Brit you'd cast as the driver in a Range Rover commercial. In the world of ad agencies, his impeccable eye for design and color is legendary. According to the legend, he once fired the entire design team because of a dispute over gunmetal gray versus dark smoke gray. Simon's agency, 12 Kings, is one of the most interesting, influential, and progressive ad firms in the world. Their slogan is "We push past the point of disruption."

Translation: "We're too cool for school."

"Could you hop over the pond straightaway and put us right?" Simon asked. I hesitated because I knew how much he hated bringing in outside help (especially from an American). There was an awkward silence as he trailed off. Finally, he spoke up again: "I'll fly you first cabin, British Airways." Now he was talking my language.

And so, thirty-three hours later, after an eleven-hour flight and a night at the Savoy, I poured over the Volka marketing materials Simon had sent me. Volka was an industrial giant who manufactured cars, trains, and construction equipment, so any mid-sized agency would want this account. To figure out the problem with Volka, I was chauffeured to 12 Kings' headquarters, where I waited to meet Simon the Great to discuss where and how he'd messed up.

The lobby of 12 Kings was like nothing else out there, with furniture in a retro-tech color palette of sky blue, sea-foam green, and Navajo white. At the center of the whole Bauhaus-inspired bête noire was an exposed plywood interior tunnel, offset and tilted 20 degrees, like some kind of interactive metaphor for the path less taken.

"The mood board that inspired this space was about gravity, vortex, action, and illusion," a junior account executive told me as she led me into the tunnel, heading toward the conference room where Simon and his team were in session.

"Mission accomplished," I said, and then had to fight my way through some high-concept plastic entry flaps (like they have at ice hockey rinks) to greet Simon, who grimly welcomed me on the other side. He wasted no time, and thrust me straight into the staff meeting.

"I'd like to introduce you all to Oren Klaff," Simon said, putting a welcoming hand on my shoulder. "Oren is *American.*" He paused, as if my American-ness implied a whole host of positives and negatives and his listeners needed a few seconds to absorb them all. "I've asked Oren here today to give us his thoughts on how we lost Volka. Oren?" And just like that, the spotlight was on me.

"Thanks, Simon." I glanced around the room. It was a midsize conference room. Like the lobby, it was the pinnacle of creative effort, complete with metal sculptures for chairs and a table made from the door of an actual castle. There were thirty-five executives in the room, some still damp from the morning rainstorm, all looking glum. "I'm glad we could get together this morning," I said, smiling. "I love London. One of my favorite cities, except when it's raining." I waited for a laugh from the crowd of soggy people in front of me, but nobody cracked a smile. Tough room. They had just lost a huge account, which meant no bragging rights at the annual awards and no annual bonus. These people thought they were attending a funeral, but I was about to tell them the patient lived.

"To get started," I said calmly, "let's flip the script, and not call this a lost account. You haven't completely lost it. At least, not yet."

"Terrific, that's terrific," Simon stated, struggling to sit upright on a polished metal bench. He needed the staff to hear this, and understand that all hope was not lost.

"Seriously," I said. "I think we can convince Volka Motors UK to take another look at the decision, and I think the outcome might be different this time, if you're willing to listen to me and act on what I say. But, fair warning: You're going to hear some things you might not like. And I'm going to ask you to do some things that might seem counterintuitive. It can be an uncomfortable process." Now we were going to see just how disruptive this agency really was. Could they truly embrace change?

A murmur of skepticism spread throughout the room, rising to an anticlimactic but distinctly English group grumble. It was still a glum party, but I also heard something else: attention. I had given them hope.

"Please, enlighten us," said Simon. I recognized a bit of pessimism in his voice.

"Let's begin. First and foremost," I said, "you guys are way too creative. Creatives are the guys always making mood boards and talking about how to 'take it to the next level,' about 'blue-sky thinking,' 'tentpole ideas,' and how 'data is the new oil.' We can't get caught in those creative clichés. Yes, I know it's hard to hear, but if we want to win this account back, we're going to be all about the money."

"Forgive me, Oren," said Brian, the director of emerging media, uncomprehendingly, "but we have to worry about creative. We're up against Bradford. They have us beat on every other front. Creativity is the ground we stand on. We have to be defined by a restlessness where the creative process never stops."

"We're not here for that. If Volka wanted an ad agency to create mood boards and name custom colors and quote dead poets, they would have hired us already. Volka doesn't want poetry; they want profit."

That got through.

"You think Bradford tried to impress them with a radically innovative marketing campaign idea?" I continued. "No, they probably came up with a pitch that sounded like this: 'We're the car advertising experts and we're going to deliver five hundred million euros in new global sales to your brand.' . . . Five hundred million. Notice anything about that number? First of all, it's a number, not a color. Second, it's a big number, but also conveniently a five percent increase in revenue for Volka. It's huge, but still feels doable.

That would be a massive win for a Volka UK campaign. So, of course, Volka skipped over you and went with the other guys."

I could see from the looks on their faces that I was speaking a different and mysterious language in this space devoted to design and illusion. I was speaking the language of money, and as they were finding, money doesn't need colorful metaphors. At least one person seemed to be hearing me, though: Simon was taking mad notes in his Moleskine.

"But we already have a big idea," said Ian, the director of lightbulb moments (his actual title). Obviously, the original pitch concepts had been his.

"Oh yeah," I said, waving the packet of information I was holding. "You mean this big idea that said, 'We're the coolest agency in the world and we've won a thousand prestigious French awards and we invented Pantomime Blue'? This is the worst thing ever. Let me explain something to you about ad agencies. To regular people, nobody really can tell the difference between any of you guys. 'We are a full-service integrated marketing agency,'" I read, hurling their own meaningless selling points back at them. "'We collaborate with our clients.' 'We've been in business for ten years and have more than a hundred and fifty years of combined management experience.'"

I tossed the materials down on the table.

"These are forgettable statements that anyone could make. These kinds of claims make it more difficult to figure out whether one agency is better than another. And so it just boils down to the money. So please, guys, put away your charcoal pencils. Put away the mood board too. If you love creativity that much, go write a graphic novel. Our job here is not that hard. All we need to do is find clear, persuasive concepts for the client, win back the account and get a ten-million-dollar budget approved."

"So what can we say to get them to reconsider our bid?" Simon asked, breaking the nervous silence. It takes a strong leader to ask a question that vulnerable in front of his team. I was impressed.

"You need to show Volka a formula for how to hire the right ad agency," I explained. "Help them understand Bradford-McCoy was the easy choice and most obvious decision, but it was still the *wrong* one. And then show them what to do about it. So how about starting a conversation like this: 'Volka, everyone agrees you need a new agency, and *if* you want to play it safe and feel like you did the 'right thing for the shareholders,' then don't overthink this decision. Just hire Bradford-McCoy, Ogilvy, Interpublic or BBDO, because any of those is a pretty good choice. Ogilvy has been around since 1948, and Interpublic about the same—and has fifty-one thousand employees. Those are huge companies with billions in revenue—Interpublic did eighteen billion last year. You hire one of those firms for the same reason you hire IBM or Boston Consulting or Goldman Sachs or Skadden Arps. They are good firms. They're convenient. No one is going to blame you if something goes wrong with that choice. You're safe.

"'But for a moment consider this: At Bradford your account will be small. They want Nestlé or Exxon or Coca-Cola. Those are the big-boy accounts. Who at a Big Five ad agency actually wants the Volka UK account? No one really. So if you hire Bradford, the team assigned to you will be getting your account as a punishment. The boss would say, "Hey Smith, Hey Johnson, get over here. You idiots screwed up big on the Ford-China account, so now I'm sticking you with Volka UK."

"'So that's it. You are now working with Smith and Johnson, the guys who screwed up on Ford-China or are fresh out of school and have never done a big campaign before. *That's* who you get from Bradford or BBDO or Interpublic. People working on your account as a punishment or a rookie assignment.

"'But for us, you're not some small-market account to be mistreated. Not at all. We'd give Volka to our most senior people, and these are people who all turned down jobs at the Big 5. Our people don't want to work on Coke or Nestlé or Exxon, because those are big, boring accounts where careers go to die. Our people want to do real ad work—they want to make advertising to sell your cars in the UK to tens of thousands of new buyers. In other words, our most senior people live and breathe and will practically die to get onto a Volka account, and they will stake their careers on doing it right.'"

I shrugged and smiled.

"Anyway," I said, "that's what I'd tell Volka."

Simon and his team were scrambling to write down every word, because I was talking fast. In reality, this was a simple Flash Roll I'd delivered a thousand times. The same script works in virtually every industry. But to Simon it was all new and fresh and exciting, and his team was eating up every word.

"Bollocks, then, let's do it," Simon said finally. "Whatever it costs. We want to hire you to win the deal back."

"OK, good," I said, just beginning to realize what I was getting myself into. "Here is what we're going to do. Simon and I are going to give the people at Volka a call and talk them into giving us another shot at the pitch. Then we are all getting on a plane, and going to spend two weeks on the ground in beautiful downtown Brinz-Prisk, near Volka headquarters, so we have a much better understanding of just what the hell it is we're trying to sell."

A SECOND BITE AT THE APPLE

In my business, usually no means no. So the first thing I was worried about was that maybe I'd been a bit too confident about how easy it would be to get a second pitch lined up. And while I was giving that "go get 'em tiger" speech, I didn't realize I was the poor SOB who was going to have to make all this actually happen. Before, I'd been talking more in the abstract. Now I would have to get to work.

I dialed the number Simon had given me, and slipped on the oversize noise-canceling Bluetooth headset with boom-mic I always wear for important calls. "Hi, Josef," I said when I got their director of marketing on the line. "This is Oren Klaff calling from 12 Kings. Listen, Simon asked me to come on board specifically to take a look at your account, because we feel we could have done better. Truth is, the first pitch meeting was rushed, and we'd like another bite at the apple."

"Didn't Simon tell you?" Josef asked in a thick Eastern European accent. "We already went in another direction. We're announcing next week."

"Yes, I understand you've decided on Bradford. But I think you ought to give us another look. We feel strongly about it. I think it's worth your while to do a quick second round meeting with us." I paused and lowered my voice slightly. "And it would be a shame if word got out in the agency world that you only give your biggest accounts to your buddies at Bradford-McCoy. Why would anybody want to waste time bidding on Volka proposals after that? I mean, why should the best new agencies bid on an account that is just going to end up at Bradford anyway? Look, I understand—if they are the *only* firm you ever want to use, then go ahead. . . . But think about it this way for a moment . . ."

Then I started speaking at a faster pace and used the same Flash Roll I'd given Simon. "At Bradford, your account would be small . . ."

From there I went into the full pitch, giving all the necessary details and industry jargon and then my suggested solution.

There were a tense few moments of silence. Surprisingly, Josef made only light-duty protests before he agreed with me. "OK, we can accept a second review; that's a reasonable request. On our end, all the key decision makers will be together in six days for a quarterly meeting at the factory headquarters," he told me. "If you have prepared a better pitch, this will be the time to present it."

"Thank you, Josef," I said. "That would be perfect." I hung up the phone and immediately called Simon over. "We're on. But we only have six days to prepare, not a few weeks. Let's take our team to Prague, ASAP—and book the economy seats, please."

"The cheap seats are pure torture," Simon said irritably.

"Yes, I know," I said. "But we're trying to win Volka, not Rolls-Royce, so we go economy all the way."

WELCOME TO BOHEMIA

The picturesque city of Brinz-Prisk, nestled along the lush banks of the Jizera River, is located in the heart of Bohemia, about eighty miles from Prague. It's hard to find any aspect of the city that hasn't been heavily influenced by Volka, and it's hard to miss the Volka factory when you arrive in the city. The auto manufacturer had a major hand in the development of the Czech Republic's economy and culture over the past hundred years.

In the nineteenth century, the town was known as Jerusalem on the Jizera, and there is a sixteenth-century Jewish cemetery that still exists inside the city limits. The town itself was named for the ancient castle Brinz-Prisk, which still towers over the city from atop the ghostly Rhube Rocks. You'll also find Catholic monuments, Roman architecture, plenty of bars and beer by the barrelful, and a peculiar local penchant for modern-day jousting, which I don't understand at all.

Of the top ten things to do in the city, five involve the Volka factory, three involve church, and the remaining two are bars. And then, of course, there is jousting. They also have a leaning tower, which isn't as famous as the one in Pisa, even though it's about to topple over. Basically, Brinz-Prisk is a manufacturing town in a romantic, old European setting.

Simon, three of the 12 Kings "disruptive geniuses," and I landed at Václav Havel Airport Prague. We were two and a half hours behind schedule, and they were out of cars at the airport, so we hailed a couple of Liftago's and hit the road. We toured the Volka museum, the factory, and even the gift shops. Everywhere we went, we learned more about the company's backstory.

We learned Volka is a proud brand, with deep roots that represent the history and aspirations of the Czech Republic. In the past, Volka had made all the "world's worst cars" lists, yet it's one of motoring's most unkillable companies. The Czech-based marque has been making cars for a hundred years, a feat equaled by only a handful of automotive firms. Anyone familiar with the design and quality of Eastern Bloc cars might wonder how Volka, of all brands, managed to stay in business while hundreds of "better" automotive companies bought the farm. And Volka hasn't just survived, but has thrived over the years, selling more than twenty-five million cars.

Volka's founders were a welder and a gunmaker. They started off manufacturing bicycles and guns in 1895, and switched to their first automobiles a decade later. The Volka 200 looked like a cross between a lawn mower and wheelbarrow and topped out at a dizzying 40 mph—so these were not cars that you bought for speed or looks. But it was beautifully constructed and, man, was it *tough*. From the beginning Volka vehicles were defined by economy, efficiency, and sturdiness. They were not the fanciest car in town, but they were the most sensible and the most reliable, much like Czechs themselves.

From 1948 to 1991, when the Soviet Union's Iron Curtain was draped around Czechoslovakia, Volka came under government control. During that period, the brand quality and creativity fell far behind Western automotive standards.

Then, in 2012, Wolfgang Schmidt took over as Volka's CEO. Schmidt, a former mechanic, was the sales and marketing director at Porsche. This was the guy we would have to convince if we wanted to pull this account away from Bradford-McCoy. He was dedicated to making Volka a dynamic global company, a shining representative of the Czech Republic—and establishing Bohemia as one of the cradles of European automobile manufacturing innovation. He could achieve his vision only by making a breakthrough in the consumer's mind about Volka, which led him to search for a brilliant ad agency to pull it off. Convince Schmidt, and all other decision makers would fall in line. He was our target.

That night, in what was considered the third-nicest hotel in the city but was really more reminiscent of a college dorm, our team was lying around the living room drinking beer, exhausted from a long day of traveling but in good spirits.

I had my laptop open and was starting to write down some ideas for the new pitch. "I'm tougher than I look," I said, typing as I spoke. "Volka is a way of telling people that I'm practical, not cheap. I'm tough, and in this world, I either find a way, or make one." Then I paused and looked up. A very bad thought had entered my mind. "All these guys speak English, right?" I asked. "What level of vocabulary can I use during this pitch—third grade, college, MBA?"

Silence. Nobody answered me.

"Hello?" I prodded.

Finally, Jonathan, 12 Kings' top copywriter, spoke up. "Oren, this is a Czech client. Has to be done in Czech."

My heart sank. This was certainly bad news. "So who gave the pitch last time?" I asked.

Trevor raised his hand. As the head of finance and accounting, he hadn't spoken much until now. "I speak German, Czech, all that stuff," he stated proudly. "I can do it, no problem."

The accountant? "No offense," I said. "You seem like a nice guy, but I'm not sure you're our best option here."

Trevor had a nervous demeanor, wrung his hands while talking, and said "umm" a lot. Could I train him to deliver our master presentation? Sure I could. But it would take three weeks—not three days.

"I need someone with acting talent, someone with poise and calm, with a presence." Had I said that aloud?

Before Trevor could register what I'd said and feel insulted, Jonathan pointed at the TV screen and said, "Someone like that guy."

We couldn't figure out how to change the channel from the Czech soap opera playing on the TV, and had left it on in the background. Jonathan was pointing at the star of the show, a heartthrob businessman type who at that moment was wowing a room of other business types with some kind of impassioned speech— no idea what it was about. I had to admit, Jonathan was right. That was the kind of guy we needed. A warm face with cool blue eyes, a voice that could read the phone book and make it sound interesting, someone who could learn the script, deliver the lines, stick to the plan, and do it all in the local language.

A thought struck me. "I mean, it's Czech Republic TV," I said. "There's no SAG or AFTRA [American Federation of Television and Radio Artists]. How much could it possibly cost to hire this guy for a few days?"

Catching on quickly, Jonathan agreed we had to throw some serious money at this problem. He said, "Yeah, let's find him, buy him out for the week, pay him ten thousand, twenty thousand— whatever, who cares? The meeting is on Friday; we need this!"

With a bit of quick googling, I found his agent, and a short while and two thousand euros later we had hired Lukas, the best actor in the Czech Republic (at least as far as we were concerned).

Now that we had officially hired an actor who knew nothing about pitching or advertising or Volka manufacturing, I had three days to prepare him to be in front of a huge client, where he would need to tell our story, deliver a complicated pitch, and negotiate a 10 million euro advertising account for Volka UK, an account we had already lost a week ago.

"I need a coffee," Simon said.

I was thinking, "Move over, coffee, this is a job for alcohol."

A SURPRISE IN THE WAITING ROOM

The Volka factory is a giant facility sprawled across the otherwise motionless meadowlands of the Czech Republic. The plant itself is organized and clean in a way that only Eastern Europeans can conceive, with spotless white pine floors and gleaming assembly lines. As we walked in, I glanced through an open doorway to the factory floor, where conveyer belts carried half-built vehicles past assembly and inspection stations. Men and women in white jump-suits examined every detail, testing every aspect of the machinery. The place was literally humming.

The executive offices were in the south end of the factory, in a building that looked a lot like the entrance to any building you might find somewhere more familiar, like New Jersey, only this had better landscaping and reliable trash removal.

Leading our team was Lukas, our Czech soap star.

The past three days had been a whirlwind. I'd spent every wak-ing minute with Lukas and I was completely burnt out. In person, the guy was nothing like his businessman personality on TV. He talked incomprehensibly fast and said, "Please, you know what I mean?" every two seconds. He would argue with a point I was making, then would scowl and pout for an hour. Then he was happy and easygoing, until the next meltdown. It was the opposite of what I needed.

Every time I attempted to lead him on a training exercise, it turned into a lengthy ordeal as he monologued about the importance of "method acting" and needing to know the motivation of his character so he was perfectly in sync with the actions and reactions of the story's antagonist—so the plot's rising action would correctly *climax* in a moment of *gravitas* leading to an emotional *denouement* for the audience.

"Hey, buddy," I said repeatedly, "we aren't doing Shakespeare here. Let's just focus on the scripts as they are written and not get caught up with all of that." But it was no use. He claimed he could not act until he had completed his "inner work."

At one point I came dangerously close to firing him when he wouldn't stop asking me about my "true purpose" in the role-play we were doing. "My purpose is to get the money," I kept repeating. "To win the deal." Apparently that wasn't the right answer.

Anyway, as difficult as the guy was—and seriously, he was a bit nuts—in the end he was really a brilliant actor, which I will get to in a moment. And it turned out he used to drive a Volka, it was his first car, first speeding ticket, first romp in the backseat, and so on.

FIGHTING LIKE A married couple, we had practiced the key elements of the scripts over and over again during those three days, and the pitch really started coming to life.

But now it was time to put all that training to the test. As we stepped into the lobby of the Volka corporate headquarters building, our fate was in the hands of Lukas the 33-year-old temperamental Czech method actor and soap opera star.

The receptionist nodded when we introduced ourselves, and led us down a long hallway to a small but comfortable executive waiting area. The six of us—Simon, Lukas, Trevor, and I, along with two creative types—sat down on a couch right outside the CEO's office complex. Just across from us sat a pair of men in charcoal suits with tightly cropped hair and narrow ties, who exchanged knowing glances as we sat down.

"Hello, gents," Simon said, engaging the men in friendly conversation, as he does with every person he meets. "American? What brings you this way?"

"From Bradford-McCoy, New York," said one of the men. "Here to meet with Wolfgang. So you're Simon from 12 Kings, right? Well, it's my second trip to Czech Republic in two weeks, thanks to all your whining and complaining about a second pitch meeting."

Wait. Bradford guys at our pitch meeting? Before we could ask any questions, an admin poked her head through the door and waved us all in. There was nothing else to do. We stood up, along with the two guys from Bradford, and followed her into the CEO's massive offices.

The interior of the Volka executive office suite was Spartan and felt strangely empty compared to the quirky furnishings of 12 Kings' offices. It was large, and jutted out from the rest of the building so that it had windows on three sides. But we only had a few seconds to take all this in before we were shuffled over to some empty chairs and told to have a seat. The guys from Bradford sat down next to us.

"Next, we have representatives from the ad agencies here for a final decision meeting on the new campaign," a little man holding a clipboard and wearing a Volka polo shirt said, announcing us to the room. I glanced over at the men seated in the back of the office. Wolfgang was easy to spot. He sat right out front with an attitude of absolute authority. Obviously, he was the boss. Just from the body language, and having been in thousands of these kinds of meetings before, I could also make out the CFO, COO, director of marketing, and even the head of the legal department. I noticed a few board members were present as well. This was a big decision. The men nodded and looked toward us as our introduction continued: "First, we have Bradford. And second, we have . . . um . . ."—the man glanced down at his clipboard for an awkward moment—"the Kingsford agency."

"Bollocks," Simon whispered, nudging me in the ribs. "They got our name wrong."

"Who cares?" I whispered back excitedly. "At least they said it in *English*. I'll be able to do the pitch myself. We won't need to use Lukas!"

Just at that moment, the executives offered some polite welcomes and the man with the clipboard waved at us to send our representative forward. One of the Bradford-McCoy men stood up and strode toward the first podium. Oh, God. This was high school debate club all over again. I got up, heart thumping in chest, and stepped over to my assigned podium.

DEBATE CLUB FOR 10 MILLION EUROS

"Why should we pick your firm to create our new UK ad campaign?" Wolfgang asked, gesturing toward the man from Bradford.

"Thank you, I'm Kevin, representing Bradford-McCoy," he said with a confident smile. "As one of the largest, most well-established marketing firms with major offices in London and New York, we are excited to partner with Volka on this fantastic project. We think you have been an Eastern European brand for far too long and we want to make you more well-known in the West, including the UK. We want to show Western Europe how a Volka automobile meets their needs. So stop hogging all of that greatness for yourselves. Let us reserve you a seat at the global commerce table with the big guys. We have a plan that will serve up another half billion in revenue for you, within twelve months."

I glanced at Simon and he was sitting stiffly, tight-lipped with arms crossed, because I had been 100 percent right about Bradford's pitch and now he knew it. These guys didn't talk about how creative they were or how many awards they had won or what colors they had invented. They spoke the language of money. No time to gloat at being right again, though, because Kevin continued to give a very credible presentation about market size,

PUT IT ALL ON THE LINE TO WIN AN IMPOSSIBLE DEAL

cost-per-customer acquisition, advertising metrics, KPIs, and return on investment.

Eventually, his presentation petered out and I was up to make the rebuttal.

"Hi, I'm Oren," I began, "with 12 Kings. I hope you take my comments in the spirit they are intended, because I think the Bradford plan we all just heard will take Volka in completely the wrong direction."

I saw them looking at me skeptically. As the losers of the previous pitch, we were starting off in a handicapped position, so I knew it would be especially important to open with status alignment. "Think about it for moment," I said, and pointed at the Bradford team. "They want to adapt your cars and your brand to fit European values. But what is so good about Western European values? Seriously, not much. We think Western European values are in decay. Oh, I get it—England, Germany, France are the nations who made the modern world truly modern and ushered humankind into the great cultural Renaissance. Sure, these countries gave us the *Mona Lisa*, *Romeo and Juliet*, Beethoven's Fifth, and a bunch of other cultural achievements. But all that happened centuries ago. Today, the sun is rising in the East, and Western aesthetic values and moral values are fading fast. In the UK, most every consumer product is fifty percent or one hundred percent made in China, which is to say it's designed by a computer, made cheaply as possible, and meant to be thrown away in a year. Clocks and watches are digital, books are read online, business meeting attire is sneakers and a T-shirt. Dinner is ordered on an app and

| 217 |

arrives in a cardboard box. Millennials in the UK don't even want cars. Most of them are not going to get a driver's license."

I was starting to get nods of approval from the men in the room. *Bingo*, a little Status Alignment achieved. These men felt like I understood them, that the West was not superior to the East. Now I would move to the next step using another flipped script. I'd have to pitch their own brand to them to demonstrate my deep understanding of their company, culture, and product.

"Why attach ourselves to Western European values?" I asked. "Instead we should be exporting Czech values. Let me explain. No one should try to make you look cooler or hipper than you are, or to reinvent your brand at all. In my experience, that's very risky. Sometimes it works out. Most of the time, it doesn't. The best campaign for Volka is one that's simple and Plain Vanilla. We have prepared a pitch that new customers will recognize immediately because it captures what has made your brand great for a hundred years, and I might tell a prospective Volka owner something like this:

"Driving a Volka is a way of telling people, I'm practical, not cheap. I'm tough, and I'm the kind of person who can either find a way, or make one. I'm reliable. I may not be from the Czech Republic, but my values sure match, because I have an inner strength I don't need to show off. I'm strong and I'm uncomplicated. My life has just two purposes: work and family. When I'm working, I do my business without a fuss, I deal with the things that come across my path, and people can rely on me. At home, we are not too fancy, we tell each other the truth, we make time for each other and appreciate what God has provided.

"Driving a Volka is not a flashy thing to do. Volka cars are not designed by futuristic robots and 3-D lasers from China. They are designed using pencils, paper, and clay models that are carefully sculpted by Bohemian craftsmen. People might think our designers are too old, drink beer that is too dark, and take too many smoke breaks. But we like them exactly for these reasons, and because they don't design the swoopiest, shiniest, coolest-looking car in the world. I think Kia does that just fine, which is why their marketing depends on singing hamsters. Instead, the people in this room are designing a car like the one my dad would have bought—except with better brakes, a more reliable engine, and better overall features to keep the passengers safe.

"This is the car my family would want me to have; it's the car my dad would have bought me. It's made the old way, but with new stuff that makes it even better. *That's* a Volka. It might look utilitarian, but it has brakes that could stop a dump truck, a heater that works at the North Pole, and a motor that never quits. Go anywhere, do anything without a complaint—experience your adventures without having to worry about the machine that's taking you there."

I glanced at the man with the clipboard and he gestured to his wrist. Time to wrap it up. I had to find a way to wrestle this account out of Bradford's hands into ours and decided on giving a quick Buyer's Formula.

"I know you asked what we can do for you in the UK," I said, getting to the point. "Sure, we can promise you five hundred million euros in new sales . . . we can promise a billion euros too. But the number has no meaning until you find the agency who understands your brand and can communicate with your customers. I'd ask you a question: How would the average worker on your production line sell a car? I'm talking about the guy on the floor who is actually putting the cars together. What does Volka mean to him? That's what the campaign needs to say and that's what the agency who creates your UK campaign needs to understand.

"The workers will know how to talk about the cars. The agency's job is to boil down that talk-track for consumers in the UK. Nothing fancy. So pick the agency your workers would actually pick. At least, that's what I would do, and I've been doing this kind of thing a long time. But of course, I can't tell you what to do; you guys will obviously do whatever is best for the Company."

And I stopped talking.

It was Bradford's turn to explain how *bad* my idea was. That's how debates work. But they never got the chance.

"Yes!" Wolfgang exclaimed after barely a second had passed. "I love it! So let's do it."

"Do what?" I wondered.

With that, he jumped up out of his chair. "Come, everyone. To the factory. I want you both to explain all this to our workers directly."

I glanced over at Lukas and he was already looking back at me, eyes wide. We both knew factory workers at Volka Brinz-Prisk don't speak English and that he was going to be onstage next, which quite possibly meant we were dead.

ON THE FACTORY FLOOR AT VOLKA HQ

It was a strange scene, this huge group of executives in suits, trailing their assistants and admin staff, followed by these buttoned-up New York ad guys and, finally, Simon, me, and Lukas bringing up the rear. I was using the extra time to prepare Lukas as much as I could, whispering under my breath.

"What's your first step going to be in there?" I asked.

"Status Alignment," Lukas said. "They need to feel like I'm one of them."

"Right," I said. "And remember you're going to be talking to factory workers, not corporate executives. The Status Tip-Off will be important to show that even though you look like a corporate executive, you're really part of the local scene."

"Yes," he said, nodding. "I can do that. I know what to say." Then he reached into his pocket and pulled out a small model car. It was a Volka Speedomatic, an older model from about five years back. He smiled. "My Flash Roll. I sell them this car. And they need to buy, because Oren, I explain Winter Is Coming."

The awkward group of executives and admins and marketing people was now making its way into the main factory. We squeezed through the large sliding door and stepped right up onto the factory floor.

"One more thing," I whispered to Lukas as we followed the herd toward the front of the room. "These guys are tough-as-nails mechanics and line workers. They are going to be highly skeptical of an outsider wearing a suit, and you're wearing a really nice suit. How will you stay compelling in the face of that?"

"I don't pretend to be big shot. I'm just me, some local guy. Yes, I'm lucky guy to work for ad agency, but no, not a big shot. I stick to guns, not change story to make them happy." Lukas beamed.

Volka's CEO, Wolfgang, was getting everyone's attention now. He pressed the emergency shutdown button and brought the humming, whirring, and hissing of the factory to a stop. Each press of the button held the line up for eleven minutes, and cost twenty thousand euros. There was a small area perfect for addressing the crowd of workers, and he stepped onto a little platform, grabbing a microphone that had appeared from a helpful administrative assistant.

"Good morning," he said in Czech, his low voice booming over the small crowd. "These men here have come from advertising agencies. I'd like you to listen to them and help me decide which one understands us the best. Which one of these firms should we hire to tell the UK and maybe even all Western Europe about Volka? Today, I want you to help make the decision."

Wolfgang gestured toward us to send our representatives forward. I nudged Lukas and he jogged over and climbed up to the platform. He grabbed the microphone with a smile and, unbelievably, followed his training. He started his Status Tip-Off, Czech-style as Trevor translated for me.

"Hi. My name is Lukas. I got my first car when I was eighteen. The parking brake didn't work, the alarm went off when it rained, and you had to kick the trunk twice to get it to open. Oh yeah, and it only came in two colors. I had the best one: red. But that car was special because it started every time, *no matter what*. And one time a police officer borrowed *my* car because *his* car was stuck in the mud and I was driving around with no problem. Do I really have to tell you what model of car it was?"

"The Kovat 480!" someone shouted.

"Yeah, the 480," came a few dozen echoes, because every Kovat 480 had the same story and only someone who grew up driving in the Czech Republic would know about the brake, that damn alarm, and the double-kick rear trunk—and how red was the best color.

"That's right," Lukas said. "The 480 was the toughest damn thing on four wheels short of a tank."

A low murmur rose up from the workers gathered around the platform. Heads started to nod vigorously. I smiled. Nodding heads and leaning in are always clear signs that Status Alignment has been achieved. I was loving this. Lukas was right on schedule, like he'd been doing this kind of presentation for years.

Now that we had their attention, it was time for Lukas's Flash Roll. He drew a deep breath and launched, rapid-fire: "Today, your best quality car is the Volka Láska 100, but it has more than thirty competitors! Even though it's not the cheapest small car out there— that's the Nissan Versa—it costs less to buy than the Ford Fiesta or VW Polo, and what's amazing is you still deliver the Láska with alloy wheels, air-con, digital radio, rear parking sensors, automatic emergency braking, and a leather steering wheel. It's impressive. Sure, I know some of your competition offer fancier technology, but as a safe, dependable supermini, the Láska is very hard to fault. Your real advantage over the other superminis is horsepower. I know you're still selling the 74 horsepower non-turbo three-cylinder Láska to the older people and the boosted 1 liter Tuned Port Injection in 94 horsepower trim to commuters—the 94 horse version is the one I like to drive. But you really caught the attention of the younger generation with the supercharged 108 bhp horse turbo in the seven-speed twin-clutch DSG automatic. If we could convince you to add a rear spoiler, front air intakes, and a lumpier camshaft— say we get 115 horsepower—we'd have a solid shot at another 250 million euros of annual sales in the supermini segment."

Man, what a Flash Roll! The guy was a champion. After this speech, the crowd was silent, no jeers or heckles. That's usually a sign that the buyers have accepted your authority and expertise in the subject. You have instilled certainty in the listener. From here on out, they won't interrupt or waste your time. With this kind of rapt attention from the buyer, it's time to deliver the Pre-Wired Ideas: Winter Is Coming, 2X, and Skin in the Game. I was on the edge of my seat, waiting to see how Lukas was going to pull it off. It was hard to follow perfectly because, again, Trevor the accountant had to translate everything for me, but this is pretty accurate for what Lukas said next about how Winter Is Coming.

"For 120 years your competitors have tried to discredit you, to outsell you, to take your customers, and they have succeeded from time to time, but they never succeeded in building a tougher car than you. So 750 of those competitors are now in the junkyard of history and you're still here, making the Láska, Vik, Zipp, and Basecamp. Today, after making twenty-five million cars . . . Volka is one of the most important manufacturers in the world! But you cannot relax, because now, some real competitors are coming for you fast and they're out for blood.

"On one end, the Koreans are coming. They sold 1.3 million cars last year and they want all your customers. Not some—*all of them*. Volka has never faced a smart, rich, and aggressive global competitor like this. But it gets worse, because coming from the other direction is BMW. They're trying to build a submini that will eat the entire segment. If we get caught between Kia and BMW, it will not be good. We will be in retreat and they will take over the market. But there's still enough time to maneuver against them by creating a clear message for UK buyers about our vehicles. We have to get that message out fast, and do it correctly, or we'll start to lose market share."

Now it was time for Lucas to get into the 2X formula.

"If we act now, I know we can *double sales* in the next five years, and we'll kick Kia all the way back to Korea. And BMW will walk away wishing they'd never heard the words *submini* or *Volka*.

"What kind of advertising message will do this? What can we tell consumers to avoid the frontal attack by Kia and the rear assault by BMW? What marketing will double sales in just a few years? Today, we have a very good ad campaign ready to launch, but it will take a little time to test, refine, and make it perfect. Give us that time.

"Why us? In the next six months, we will dedicate *all* of our *key staff* to making this campaign work. In other words, we will be *all in*. No other agency can offer that level of commitment. We will fight Kia. We will send BMW back to Bavaria. Together we will double your sales. This is how we fight—together—because I would rather die on my feet fighting with you against Kia than live on my knees, watching them take the UK market. *And I know you feel the same way.*"

Shouts went up from the workers as Lukas finished. A few fists were thrust into the air. This resonated with them, of course, because Lukas was describing their brand in a way that they would have described it to their friends or even a person who knows nothing about cars. He was touching on the values that already resonated with them. It was all very Plain Vanilla. But if we wanted to cement our status as the clear choice, we couldn't be *entirely* Plain Vanilla. We'd have to show these workers that we were also offering to take them into the new normal, that we were different from everyone else in one key way.

"In the past, consumers chose a car by its reputation. Volvos were safe. A Toyota lasts forever. BMWs are fun to drive. Mercedeses are classy. Jeeps go anywhere. Hondas sip gas. But today, things are different. Consumers have discovered that all cars are good, efficient, fun to drive, and super safe. There isn't a bad car out there. Believe it or not, a Pontiac is as safe as a Volvo. And the cost from one model to the next is similar. The supposed differences between brands have mostly become myths. *Quality* is the new normal. It's the same with Volka: Your cars are high quality, have advanced technology, and are extremely safe and low-cost to operate. But so are others. So in the consumer's mind, you are just another car, very similar to Toyota, Nissan, VW, and Hyundai. *Except* . . . for one big difference. A Volka is tough. This is a *real* difference that Western Europeans can understand and appreciate. More than any other car, we are practical, honest, and tough. So if you want a high-quality car with all the features and performance of any other car, but you want something *functional and tough*, then you want a Volka."

I continued to be impressed. Lukas had obviously been practicing for this moment during the off hours, and a star was born. He had expertly framed our offer as Plain Vanilla with just one unique element. He showed them that we could become the new normal for a big part of the UK market. But he wasn't done yet. It was almost time to invite pessimism and ask the buyers to question him and the deal. But first, Lukas was going to reveal his Buyer's Formula. He was going to teach these factory workers a quick lesson on choosing an ad agency.

"I know . . . up here we're a bunch of guys in suits; we have ten minutes to talk to you, give you a few lines, make a few promises, then we all fly back to New York, London, Frankfurt, Tel Aviv . . . wherever. And you never see us again, but you still have to rely on us to help you sell cars. How are you supposed to make such a big decision in such a short amount of time? I cannot tell you *who* to choose, but since I do this kind of thing a lot, maybe I can show you *how* to choose.

"First, pick someone who has studied your 125-year history and has driven your cars. And not just the mighty flagship Basecamp but the lowly ten-thousand-euro Minimoto too. And 'driving' doesn't mean a one-hour test-drive; it means driving thousands of miles over many years. For example, I once drove my Kovat 480 to Spain and back . . . in three days!

"Second, forget how big an ad agency is, because in our world, a big agency looks like it would be the best, but big is slow—and slow is dead—meaning size hurts you instead of helping you. Third, don't pick someone you feel good about, and think you might 'like as a person' and get along with (and this might not make sense now), but pick someone you can argue with, fight with, disagree with . . . and still, even though mad and frustrated—they will show up the next day, to work. They don't show up for 'sensitivity counseling' or to talk through their feelings or to complain about you to the bosses. They just show up to do the work.

"The table stakes are high, because we're talking about the very future of Volka, so you don't want to hire prima donnas and sensitive types. If it were me, I'd pick the kind of people you can have a few drinks with, and make sure they drink Branik dark, not Corona Light."

Many heads nodded knowingly about Branik dark, possibly the best beer in the Czech Republic.

"Finally, I think you pick someone who knows cars, not car advertising. Because look at these ads—they are all the same." He held up a stack of small posters and flipped through them. "Is this an ad for Toyota or Nissan? Ford or Kia? Who knows? The right agency won't make these cliché ads, because they love cars, not advertising. Now look at this Porsche ad. You can tell they love cars. And this ad for Ford trucks. These were done by agencies like us—small agencies, people who love cars and make easy-to-understand car ads. And may God strike me down, but we will never put singing hamsters in a Volka TV commercial."

With that final dig at Kia, it was done. He stopped talking, put the microphone down, and hopped off the platform. The small crowd erupted into applause that seemed to go on and on. It took a few precious and expensive minutes to get everyone settled down enough to listen to the Kevin guy from Bradford-McCoy. And they hated him right from the start. Although he spoke some decent Czech, it sounded like he had learned it from a Rosetta Stone app on an iPad on the flight over. He came across as elitist and privileged. These factory workers weren't buying what he was selling. He had failed to achieve Status Alignment. After just a few minutes he was talking to some very bored workers. Giving the wrong speech to the wrong audience, he finally accepted defeat, slumped down off the platform, and trailed off without any real call to action. When he finished, the manufacturing line restarted and the workers were gone.

The rest is history. A few hours later Simon and team were all

on a flight back to London with a signed Volka Motors UK contract for 10 million euros in hand. And Lukas had earned a place
in advertising history.

Personally, I just couldn't wait to get back home to California
to cook a large meal in my new kitchen and take my son to hockey
practice. Just be a dad for a little while and slow things down.
Yeah, that was going to be nice.

Simon had pulled the Volka card on me, same as I had on him,
claiming the rules "forced" him to book me an economy ticket on
the return flight to the States, so I leaned back and snuggled into
the world's most uncomfortable seat, then glanced down at my
phone as a new text message came in. It was from an unknown
number but the sender clearly knew who I was.

"Oren. Confidential deal. $40 million. I'm in Boston tomorrow.
See attached file. You in or out?" That was all it said.

I had to admit, I was intrigued. Was it Anton? John King?
Logan? Billy?

"Who's this?" I texted back.

"Mike Bixby," came the immediate reply.

OK, that got my attention. He was the CEO of Hyperloop, the
revolutionary transportation company that was worth almost a
billion dollars.

"I'm IN. See you there," I typed. Then I paused, my finger over
the Send key.

I took a breath. I thought about my little boy back home, and
my beautiful wife who missed the heck out of me (if her recent
texts were to be believed). Too many deals lately. It was starting

to take a toll. I tried to remember the last time I'd been home for two weeks straight. It had just been deals, deals, deals. Maybe one too many.

I deleted my first message and wrote, "Sorry Mike. Love to, but I'll have to catch you on the next one. I'm Out." Then I put the phone into airplane mode. This time, I was going to keep it there.

CONCLUSION

IT'S YOUR TURN

You've seen how I used these principles in high-stakes situations to land important deals without pressuring or coercing the buyers. With a little practice, you'll soon be doing the same.

Since developing this set of techniques, I've taught it to thousands of people—and regardless of their skill level or experience, I've watched them apply this approach, flip the script, and achieve inception in their deals. They've been astounded by the results, and so have I.

So here's a quick recap of the process; think of it as a quickstart guide:

You'll start by getting your audience—whether they're a buyer, an investor, or a business partner—to pay full attention to you and take you seriously, as they would a partner or colleague. And you'll do this by achieving Status Alignment, the first step to making a deal.

No buyer of any kind is going to listen to you until they feel they're in the right place at the right time with the right person. That's why the Status Tip-Off is so powerful. When your buyer sees that you understand who they are, can speak their language, and are part of their in-group, they'll immediately become receptive to what you have to say. Whether you're talking to an assembly line worker or the CEO of the company, you need to establish that you fit right into their world.

Either way, a Status Tip-Off works the same—it's a brief story or phrase that would be known only by an in-group member and will instantly cement your status as "one of us."

But achieving Status Alignment is not enough to make a deal happen. You probably have friends whom you trust and respect. However, how many of them would you hire to manage and invest your money?

When the stakes are high, you need to instill absolute Certainty in the buyer's mind that you're a true expert in your field and that things will happen exactly as you say they will. To do this, you're going to use a Flash Roll.

While the Status Tip-Off aligns you with your audience by showing them you have a lot in common, the Flash Roll should distance you from your audience, demonstrating your technical expertise in one very specific field—which happens to be the area in which they are having a difficult problem.

Once you've established your Status and expertise, it's time to explain your big idea to the buyer. Specifically, to answer the three questions in the buyer's mind: Why do I care? What's in it for me? and Why you? The faster you answer these, and the less cognitive strain you place on the buyer, the better your chances are of closing the deal. The easiest way to do this is using a sequence of Pre-Wired Ideas:

- Winter Is Coming
- 2X
- Skin in the Game

These ideas are designed to fit into the deepest pre-wired idea receptors in the human brain while supplying your audience with the answers they need to move forward with you. With Pre-Wired Ideas, your audience will understand everything they need to know about you and what you're offering.

But you don't just want your buyer to understand your idea, you want them to buy in and pitch it back to you—to invite you into your own deal. You want to flip the script. And this isn't going to happen until the buyer feels safe to explore your idea more deeply and entertain both the positives and the potential negatives.

To make the buyer feel interested enough to explore a new idea but safe enough to move forward, you need to find their novelty sweet spot. Show them how your offer is the New Normal—a Plain Vanilla concept with just one key and valuable difference. To keep things moving along, you should lump together all of the ways your product or idea is new and unique so the buyer isn't overwhelmed or scared to buy it. Then show how your offer is new and different from the status quo in just one key way. If you're in a room full of Czech business executives as I was, you can tell them you're exactly the same as the top ten creative agencies in the world, but much smaller (and therefore more effective).

By this point, the buyer is becoming attracted to your idea and the idea of working with you, and you won't feel the need to control, pressure, or corner them. Instead, you'll be in free exchange of ideas and plans to move forward.

However, before you actually turn the power to make the decision over to your buyer, there's one final step: You need to contain their pessimism within a set of pre-defined boundaries. I call this an invisible fence. To do this, use a Buyer's Formula to teach them how to buy whatever you're selling.

When you list the obvious ways to fail before you relinquish control to the buyer, you block off certain options in their mind, like when you tell a late-career athlete about the common mistakes made by other big name late-career athletes or when you tell a car company about the obvious mistakes in hiring a car advertising firm that can cost millions. That's why it's so important to build Alignment and Certainty, so you are credible, believable, and in position as the world's best expert in the buyer's specific problem.

One note of caution: Through the above five steps, you can't change who you are or change your values to make the buyer happy. One reason why so many people are mistrustful of salespeople is because they see the seller move through different characters during a sales pitch, and this leaves buyers feeling confused and uncertain. Flipping the script isn't about changing yourself to give the buyer what they want; it's about sticking to your guns. Stay consistent to your personality, your character, and most importantly, your values. This is what the most compelling people in the world have that others don't: character and values.

In the final delivery of your ideas, if you're considered an insider and an expert, if the buyer knows why they should care about your idea, what's in it for them, and why you; if you acknowledge their concerns or objections, and guide them through the process of buying your product; and in all this they find you to be a compelling person, they will search for, find, and suggest a way to do business with you.

It can be nerve-racking to attempt Inception, especially when you give autonomy to the buyer to make his own decision. This pressure intensifies when you're dealing with someone with a lot more power than you, or if you're stuck on a team that's used to doing things the old way. In these scenarios, it can feel tempting to fall back on the old sales methods you're used to. You have to resist this temptation. While it feels safe to resort to your old argumentative sales methods (because everyone feels like they have "a shot at closing" when trying to overcome the buyer's objections), doing so will undermine any progress you've made towards encouraging your buyer to work with you.

If you stick to the steps and practice your delivery, you'll be flipping the script, incepting ideas into the buyer's mind, and stacking up many financial wins and social rewards.

Soon, the people you want to work with will find their way to you, start pitching you on the idea of getting together, and doing a deal.

CONCLUSION

If you want to join me in one more adventure, I invite you to read *the lost chapter*, an important story and set of methods that didn't make the publishing deadline of this book but definitely should be read.

You can read it at orenklaff.com/flip.